Developing ICT Skills

Information and Communication Technology

KEY STAGE 1: RECEPTION/YEAR 1 PRIMARY 1/2

Frances Mackay

HOPSCOTCH EDUCATIONAL PUBLISHING

Contents

Page	Lesson	DfEE IT SoW	New NC IT ATs	Other curriculum links
6 - 9	1 Introducing the computer		5c	Literacy Framework: Reception term 1, W11 Year 1 term 1, W12
10 - 13	2 Labelling	Unit 1A	2a 5c 3a 4a	Literacy Framework: Reception term 1, T 15 Year 1 term 2, T 22
14 - 17	3 Modelling	Unit 1A	2a 3b 2d 4a 3a	Art and design: 1a, 1b, 2b, 2c, 3a, 5a, 5b, 5c
18 - 21	4 Keyboard skills	Unit 1B	2d 3a 3b	Literacy Framework: Reception W3 Year 1 term 1, W2
22 - 25	5 Using a word bank	Unit 1B	2b 5c 3b 4a	Literacy Framework: Reception S1 Year 1 term 1, S4
26 - 29	6 Obtaining information	Unit 1C	1a 4a 1c 4b 2d 5b	
30 - 33	7 Presenting information	Unit 1C	3a 3b 4a	Literacy Framework: Reception T15 Year 1 term 1, T14
34 - 37	8 Sorting	Unit 1D	1c 2b 3a	Numeracy Framework: Reception 19 Year 1 90-93
28 - 41	9 Pictograms	Unit 1E	1a 2a 1b 2b 1c 3a	Numeracy Framework: Year 1 90-93
42 - 45	10 Controlling machines & devices	Unit 1F	1b 5b 3a 4a	
46 - 49	11 Sequencing instructions	Unit 1F	2c 4b 2d 5b 4a	Literacy Framework: Year 1 term 1, T13
50 - 53	12 Following instructions	Unit 1F	2c 4b 2d 4a	Literacy Framework: Year 1 term 1, T13 Numeracy Framework: Reception 27, Year 1 88 Geography: 3c
54 - 57	13 Recording instructions	Unit 1F	2c 4b 2d 4a	Literacy Framework: Year 1 term 1, T16
58 - 61	14 Predicting instructions	Unit 1F	2c 4b 2d 4a	
62 - 72	Appendix			

ICT Skills
Reception/Year 1

©Hopscotch Educational Publishing

Introduction

ABOUT THE SERIES

Developing ICT Skills is a series of books written specifically to complement the QCA and DfEE *Information Technology Scheme of Work for Key Stages 1 and 2*. There is one book for each year from Reception/Year 1 (Scottish Primary 1/2), through Key Stage 1 to Year 6 (Scottish Primary 7) at the end of Key Stage 2.

The series offers a structured approach with the non-specialist in mind and provides detailed lesson plans to teach specific ICT skills. A unique feature of the series is the provision of differentiated photocopiable activities designed to support each lesson. Most of these activities are independent tasks that can be completed away from the computer or IT equipment being used, thereby enabling the teacher to work with a focus group at the computer. The differentiation of the activities considerably reduces teacher preparation time when planning group work.

The lessons have been specifically written for the classroom with access to only one computer but will, of course, work equally well in a computer suite situation.

Accompanying each of the two books for Key Stage 1 is a CD-Rom, produced by AirCom International, that contains activities designed to support each lesson. Schools will not, therefore, need a separate word processor, art or music package, for example, to teach the ICT skills being addressed. If schools prefer to use their own computer programs, however, the books are designed to stand alone without the accompanying CD-Rom.

ABOUT THIS BOOK

This book is for teachers of Reception/Year 1 (Scottish Primary levels 1/2) children. It aims to:

- develop children's ICT skills through a series of structured lessons aimed at increasing their awareness of the strengths and limitations of ICT;
- support teachers by providing practical teaching methods and activity ideas based on whole-class, group, paired and individual teaching;
- support non-specialist teachers by providing structured lesson plans with practical ideas and 'specialist tips' designed to address some of the common problems the children (and teachers!) may experience;
- provide, where possible, cross-curricular lessons;
- encourage the children to recognise the importance of ICT in everyday experiences;
- encourage enjoyment of as well as confidence in using ICT skills.

LESSON CONTENT

Learning objectives

This sets out the specific learning objectives for each lesson.

Resources

This is a list of what you will need to do the lessons.

Whole class introduction

This provides ideas for introducing the activity, and may include key questions to ask the children, so that they can move on to their group task having learned concepts and the vocabulary they will need for the group activities.

Group activities

Focus group – with the teacher
This follows the whole class introduction and is a teaching session with the teacher working together with the children at the computer (or other ICT equipment). The teaching in this session can either be carried out with the whole class (by using a computer and a projected screen or by using a computer suite) or within a small group while the rest of the class do the photocopiable activity sheets (if appropriate) or another (sometimes related) independent task. This section contains suggestions for teaching the key concepts and skills related directly to the ICT learning objectives for the lesson. Hints and tips are provided to help support the teacher when introducing these skills. The suggestions can be used in relation to the CD-Rom that accompanies this book (at Key Stage 1) or to the teacher's own computer programs.

Using the photocopiable activity sheets
Each lesson includes three differentiated activity sheets which can be completed by the children independently of the teacher. They contain the same activity at three levels of ability so that the same task can be completed by below average, average and above average children at their own level. Activity sheet 1 tasks are the easiest and Activity sheet 3 the hardest. In most cases, the sheets contain tasks that are designed to be completed away from the computer or ICT equipment being used but reinforce the skills that will be used at the computer itself. Many activities are also designed so that the children can compare a manual task

ICT Skills
Reception/Year 1

©Hopscotch Educational Publishing

Introduction

with a computer one (editing text, for example), thereby enabling a discussion during the plenary session about the strengths and limitations of ICT.

Sometimes, the sheets can be completed immediately after the whole class introduction (so some children may be working with the teacher in a small group at the computer while the rest are completing the sheets). At other times, the sheets are to be completed only after the children have experienced the focus group session (in a classroom with only one computer, the children may need to be set other independent tasks until they have been part of the focus group).

For each lesson, then, each child should experience the whole class introduction and a focus group session as well as completing an activity sheet. In classrooms with only one computer this means the teacher may need to organise the lesson over a week, for example:

Mon	whole class introduction
	group A – with the teacher at the computer (focus group session)
	groups B, C and D – completing the activity sheets
Tues	group B – focus group session
	group A – activity sheet
	groups C and D – independent tasks
Wed	group C – focus group session
	groups A, B and D – independent tasks
Thurs	group D – focus group session
	groups A, B and C – independent tasks
	plenary – all groups

◆ Plenary session

This suggests ideas for a whole-class review to discuss the learning outcomes, and gives questions to ask so that the children have a chance to reflect on what they have learned and for the teacher to assess their knowledge and understanding. This session may not necessarily take place on the same day as the whole class introduction – it may come at the end of the week after all the children have completed their focus group session and activity sheets.

◆ APPENDIX ◆

At the back of this book are some extra photocopiable pages. Page 62 offers suggestions for how these pages could be used. Most of the pages have been prepared for the teacher to use as resources for particular lessons but there are also ideas on how to use the pages to develop further activities in follow-up sessions. Where relevant, these pages also contain the answers to particular activity sheets.

Page 72 contains an assessment sheet that outlines the basic concepts and skills that a Reception/Year 1 child should experience. This page can be photocopied for each child and, together with the work produced from each lesson, be used to compile a comprehensive individual ICT profile to make assessments and determine future targets.

◆ HARDWARE REQUIREMENTS ◆

Teachers using this book will require a Windows-based multi-media computer and colour printer as well as tape recorders.

◆ SOFTWARE REQUIREMENTS ◆

The CD-Rom that accompanies this book contains all the relevant software that the teacher will need in order to resource the lessons. However as these programs are not full versions and are only intended to be an introduction to the particular programs required, the teacher may decide to extend the children's experiences by making sure the following software is available:

✦ a WYSIWYG (What You See Is What You Get) word processor with a talking word bank facility and graphic insert capability;
✦ a program that allows text and pictures to be organised on screen;
✦ a multi-media program such as a talking book;
✦ simple adventure game(s);
✦ a painting package with stamps or motifs;
✦ a graphing package that creates pictograms.

Introduction

TEACHING ICT

For many of today's adults there has always been a degree of mystique surrounding ICT skills. Some people have even avoided contact with computers altogether! However, in the teaching profession, this is not an option. In truth, there is nothing difficult about acquiring or teaching ICT and, in fact, there has never been a better or more exciting time to become a computer user. To become a confident ICT user, whether teacher or pupil, you need to be taught a few basic skills and to become familiar with the way technology works, but you do not need to become an expert. The National Curriculum requires ICT to be taught to all pupils and this can seem daunting if the teacher is learning alongside the pupils. In this series we aim to provide the teacher with the materials, skills and knowledge that will make covering the ICT Scheme of Work an achievable and positive experience. We expect children who take part in the lessons to learn age-appropriate ICT skills and to become discerning users of technology.

Schools that teach ICT skills discretely then transfer those skills to other subject areas find that children achieve higher levels of ICT competence than when ICT skills are taught **only** through other subjects. This suggests that teachers should set aside time specifically for the teaching of ICT skills. This does not mean that it is necessary to timetable ICT lessons every week but it is important to make sure some ICT lessons are devoted to the teaching of specific ICT skills. This can be carried out through occasional whole-class lessons as well as small group or individual lessons and does not necessarily require the whole class to be working on ICT at the same time. The lessons in this book agree with this premise and ICT is the main focus of each one. However, where there are opportunities for links with other curriculum areas, advantage of this has been taken.

Prior to the publication of the QCA and DfEE IT SOW it was difficult for schools to know exactly what ICT skills should be taught to each year group. We have now been presented with a clear and comprehensive guide which clearly demonstrates continuity and progression. If you are working with older children who have not had the opportunity to acquire the rudimentary skills, it would be best to work at the correct level for these children. Hence the years and levels suggested in the IT SOW and in this series of books are to be taken as desireable guidelines.

In order to achieve a high level of success for the children, teaching intentions should be very clear and built within a whole-school scheme of work that demonstrates evident continuity and progression of concepts and skills. This is extremely important in ICT because today, perhaps more than ever before, children vary considerably in their ICT capabilities. Many children who have access to ICT outside school can appear to have greater skills in handling software and hardware but teachers need to be aware that these children may not necessarily have the full range of ICT capabilites expected of them in the programmes of study. Regular observations and assessments are therefore necessary to ascertain the best tasks and experiences to support the children's learning.

Reliability of the technology has often been one of the biggest hurdles for schools! Therefore, before you begin to use the lessons in this series, we recommend that you check that all the necessary equipment is working correctly. Access to broken or out-of-date technology is time wasting and very frustrating for teachers and children alike.

Published by Hopscotch Educational Publishing Company Ltd, 29 Waterloo Place, Leamington Spa CV32 5LA 01926 744227

© 1999 Hopscotch Educational Publishing

Written by Frances Mackay
Series consultant – Ayleen Driver
Series design by Blade Communications
Illustrated by Claire Artes
Cover illustration by Susan Hutchison
Printed by Clintplan, Southam

Frances Mackay hereby asserts her moral right to be identified as the author of this work in accordance with the Copyright, Designs and Patents Act, 1988.

ISBN 1-902239-42-3

All rights reserved. This book is sold subject to the condition that it shall not, by way of trade or otherwise, be lent, hired out or otherwise circulated without the publisher's prior consent in any form or binding or cover other than that in which it is published and without a similar condition, including this condition, being imposed upon the subsequent purchaser.

No part of this publication may be reproduced, stored in a retrieval system, or transmitted, in any form or by any means, electronic, mechanical photocopying, recording or otherwise, without the prior permission of the publisher, except where photocopying for educational purposes within the school or other educational establishment that has purchased this book is expressly permitted in the text.

Lesson 1
Introducing the computer

◆ Learning objectives

- To name the parts of a computer.
- To discuss the uses of a computer.

◆ Resources

- Computer with keyboard and mouse.
- Photocopiable page 63.

◆ Whole class introduction

- Show the computer to the children. Ask them the following questions:
  - How many of you have a computer at home?
  - Who uses the computer at home?
  - What do they use the computer to do?
  - Have you used a computer yourself?
  - What did you use the computer to do?
  - Do you know where else we might find a computer apart from in our homes?
  - What might these computers be used for?
- Discuss the different types of computers, such as hand-held computer games, those at supermarkets, bank hole-in-the-wall machines and so on.
- Tell the children about the computers you have at school. Tell them the kinds of things that might be done using the school office computer, for example. How might these things have been done before the computer was invented?
- Explain that a computer can help us in lots of different ways by making things quicker and easier but that computers are only as clever as the people who build and use them.
- Use a computer to discuss the names of its parts. What parts do the children know the names of already? Make sure they use the correct terms, such as monitor or screen, not TV, for example. As you discuss each part, use the labels on page 63 to label the computer.

◆ Group activities

Focus group – with the teacher

- With a small group at the computer, reinforce the names of the parts of the computer and attach the name labels to each part. Allow each child time to match the label to the parts and say the words.
- Tell the children briefly what each part does. If appropriate, show them how to switch the computer on and off and how to tell if the computer is on. Discuss safety issues, such as how to put the plug in the socket if they ever need to and what they should do if something goes wrong.
- Ask them to remind you about some of the things a computer can be used for.

Using the photocopiable activity sheets

- Use the activity sheets to reinforce the lesson.

◆ Plenary session

Ask someone from each group to share what they did on their activity sheet. Revise the names of the parts of the computer again and what a computer can be used for. Keep the labels on the computer for several weeks until the children are very familiar with the terms and can begin to recognise the words.

Name _____   Activity 1   Date _____

◆ The computer ◆

◆ Colour the computer.

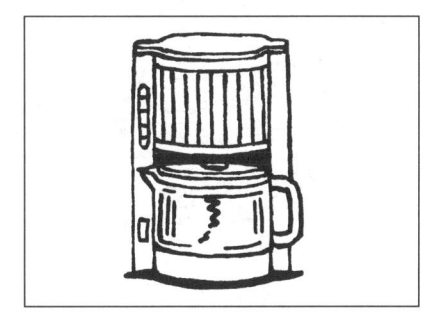

◆ Colour the keyboard.

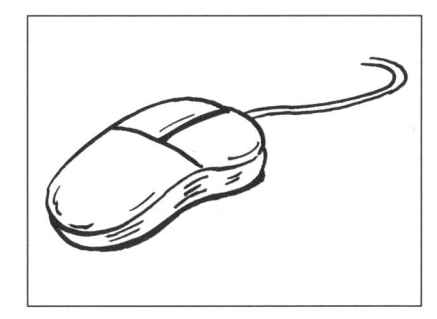

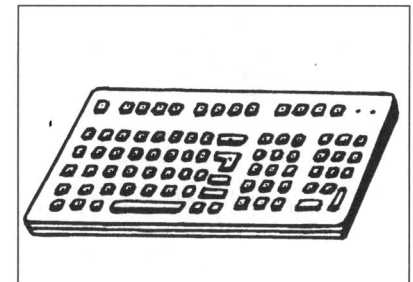

◆ Colour the mouse.

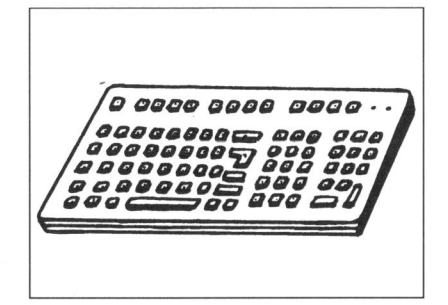

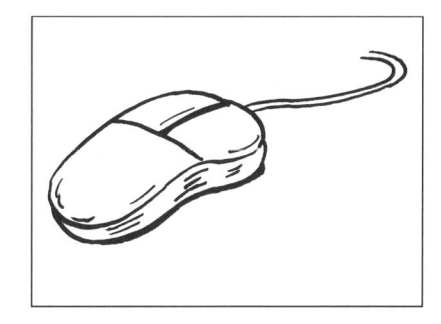

ICT Skills
Reception/Year 1

Photocopiable
©Hopscotch Educational Publishing

7

Name _____ Activity 2 Date _____

✦ The computer ✦

✦ Draw a line from the computer to the pictures that show us some of the things our school computer can be used for.

3 + 2 = 5
5 − 3 = 2

doing sums

computer

jumping

cooking

One day I went to see my friend. We played on my swing.

writing

✦ Draw a line from each word to the correct part of the computer.

keyboard

monitor

mouse

ICT Skills
Reception/Year 1

Photocopiable
©Hopscotch Educational Publishing

8

Name _____   Activity 3   Date _____

✦ The computer ✦

✦ Choose the correct word from the word box to complete these sentences about our school computer.

do	cook	clean	write
play	wash	draw	walk

We can _____ stories using our computer.

We can _____ pictures using our computer.

We can _____ sums using our computer.

We can _____ music using our computer.

✦ Choose the correct words to label this computer. Write them in the boxes.

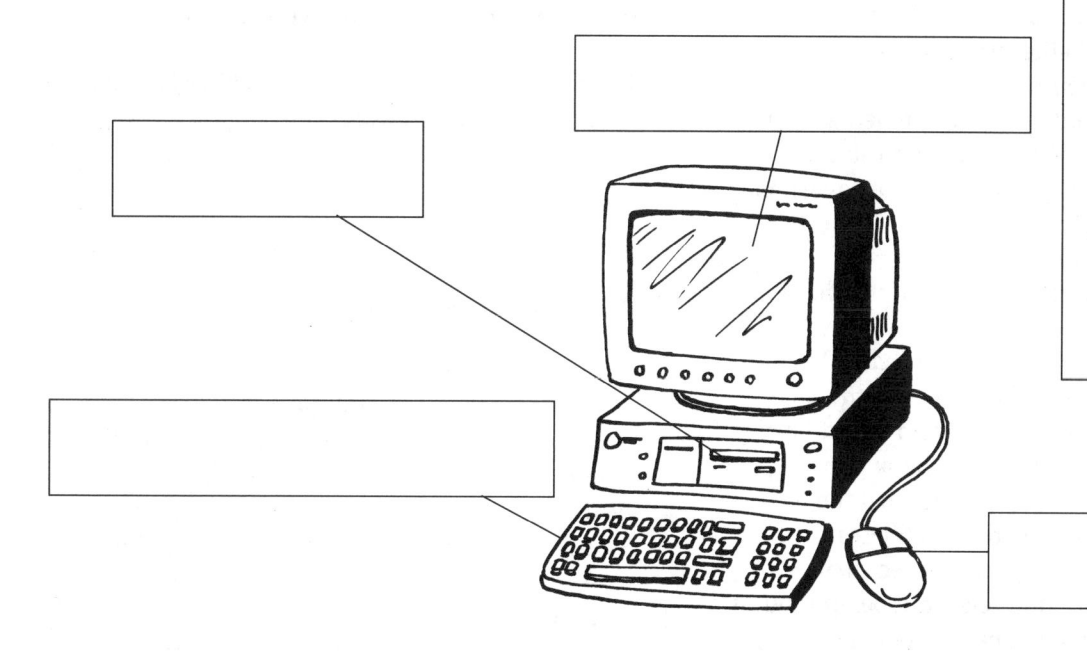

mouse
keyboard
computer
monitor
television
disc drive

ICT Skills
Reception/Year 1

Photocopiable
©Hopscotch Educational Publishing

Lesson 2

Labelling

◆ Learning objectives

- ✦ To match words to pictures.
- ✦ To know that ICT can be used to match words to pictures.
- ✦ To use a mouse to select and move items on screen.

◆ Resources

- ✦ A teacher-prepared big book with one picture and matching word on each page of a: chair, mat, bed, cooker and bath (using simple drawings, magazine pictures or photocopiable page 64).
- ✦ Pictures of a cushion, cat, teddy, pan and rubber duck (photocopiable page 64).
- ✦ Word cards for cushion, cat, teddy, pan and rubber duck.
- ✦ Aircom CD-Rom Activity 1 (a–e) and/or a computer program that allows text and pictures to be organised on screen.

◆ Whole class introduction

- ✦ Tell the children that they will be sharing a book about things they might find in a house. Cover up the words with sticky notes (or similar) before sharing the book. As you look at each picture, discuss what the item is, where it might be found in the house and whether or not the children have this item in their house.
- ✦ Uncover the first word and read it together. Could the picture have a different label and still be correct? (Could the cooker be called a stove?) Ask the children to predict the labels for the other pictures before you uncover them.
- ✦ Next, show the children the cut-out pictures of the cushion, cat, teddy, pan and duck. Ask them to tell you where they would most probably belong in the pictures in the big book. Would the duck go in the bath? Agree where each item might belong and stick the pictures on the big book pages.
- ✦ Now ask the children to help you label the pictures. Read the word cards together and display them where everyone can see them. Ask someone to come out and select a label and put it next to the correct picture in the book. Does everyone agree? Finally, re-read the big book together, including all the new labels.
- ✦ Tell the children that they are now going to do some matching and labelling of their own using an activity sheet and a computer program.

◆ Group activities

Focus group – with the teacher

- ✦ At the computer, tell the children that they will be using a program that will let them move pictures and words about, just like they did with the big book. Show them the mouse and how to hold and move it correctly on the mouse mat. Introduce the term 'cursor' or 'pointer' and explain that the mouse moves the pointer on screen. Allow time for each child to try this for themselves.
- ✦ Next, show how the mouse button can be used to click on an object or word to select it. Make sure they know which button to use (you could mark it with a sticky label). Show how moving the mouse can then move the object on screen. Match up a word to a picture by dragging. Explain that many people find moving the mouse difficult to do at first. Allow each child time to select and match words to pictures. Print out and date their work.

Using the photocopiable activity sheets

- ✦ The activity sheets could be used either before or after the computer session.

◆ Plenary session

Ask someone from each group to share what they did on their activity sheet. Ask the children to compare the activity sheet with the computer work. Which was the easiest to do? Why? Explain that it is not always easier to do a task using the computer but that sometimes a computer can help us with the presentation of our work.

Name _____ Activity 1 Date _____

✦ Things in the home ✦

✦ Match the pictures of things that belong together. One has been done for you.

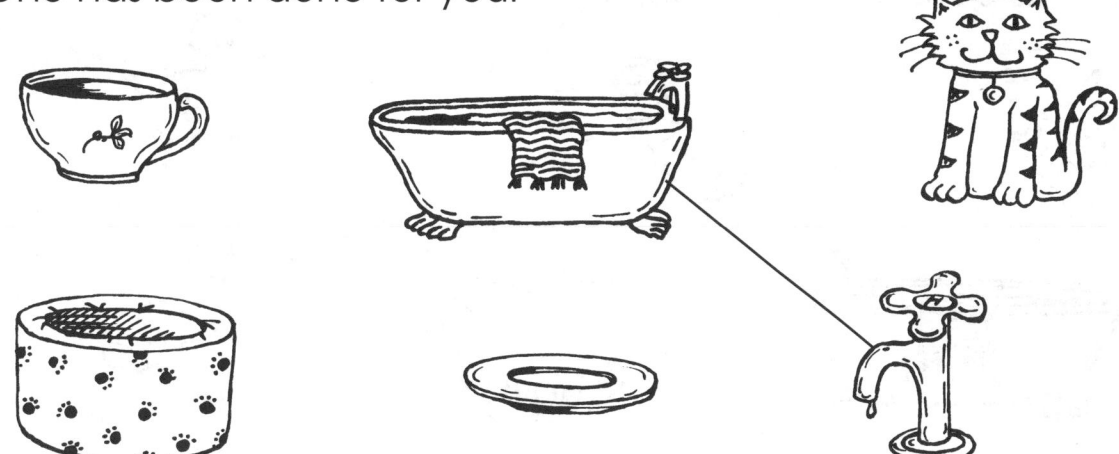

✦ Cut out the labels below. Match them to the correct picture. Then on the back of this sheet, draw and label something from your home.

| cup | mat | pan | cat | tap |

ICT Skills
Reception/Year 1

Photocopiable
©Hopscotch Educational Publishing

11

Name _____ **Activity 2** Date _____

✦ Things in the home ✦

✦ Match the pictures of things that belong together. One has been done for you.

✦ Cut out the labels. Match them to the correct picture. Then on the back of this sheet, draw and label 2 things found in your home.

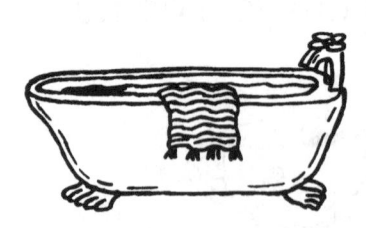

| duck | fish | bath | sock | book | door |

Name _____   Activity 3   Date _____

◆ Things in the home ◆

◆ Match the pictures of things that belong together. One has been done for you.

◆ Cut out the labels. Match them to the correct picture. Then on the back of this sheet, draw and label 3 things found in your home.

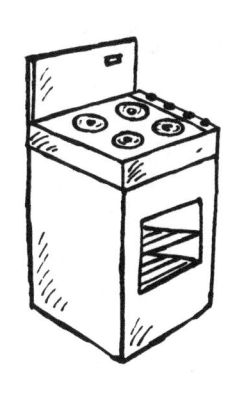

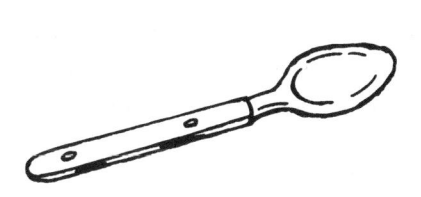

| cooker | brush | teapot | spoon | teddy | computer |

ICT Skills
Reception/Year 1

Photocopiable
©Hopscotch Educational Publishing

Lesson 3

Modelling

◆ Learning objectives

- ✦ To understand that computers can represent real or fantasy situations.
- ✦ To understand that a computer can be used to create representations of various scenarios.
- ✦ To use simple tools in a painting package.
- ✦ To add stamps/motifs to their work.
- ✦ To print out their work.

◆ Resources

- ✦ A copy of the fairy tale 'The Three Little Pigs'.
- ✦ A painting program with stamps or motifs.

◆ Whole class introduction

- ✦ Remind the children about the story of the three little pigs by sharing it with them. Discuss the three different types of houses built by the pigs. Ask them to describe what each one might have looked like. What colours would the buildings be? What things would the houses have (doors, windows, chimney, garden and so on)? What might the gardens be like?
- ✦ If the book has pictures of the houses, share these with the children. Do they look like they imagined them to be when they were listening to the story? Discuss the fact that the story is not real – it is fantasy or made up, so we can use our imagination as to what the houses might look like. Explain that this is why the pictures might be different in different books on the same story.
- ✦ Tell the children that they are going to draw pictures of the three little pigs' houses using an activity sheet and the computer.
- ✦ Use the activity sheets first. Explain that you want them to colour the pictures and add the details **they** think should be added to the houses – that is, to use their own imagination in completing the pictures.

◆ Group activities

Focus group – with the teacher

- ✦ Tell the children that computers can be used to colour pictures.
- ✦ Show them how to use simple tools in the 'Paint' package, such as 'Brush', 'Palette' and 'Colour-fill'.
- ✦ Demonstrate how to use stamps/motifs to add more complex representations to the picture.
- ✦ Show the children how to use the 'Print' tool to print out their work. Establish rules for printing, such as getting permission before printing it out.
- ✦ Allow the children time to experiment with the tools to create their own picture. It could be a different representation of the three little pigs' houses or they could draw the wolf's house!

Using the photocopiable activity sheets

- ✦ Use these before the computer session.

◆ Plenary session

Share the responses to the activity sheets and the computer session. What decisions did they have to make in both activities? What choices did that have when they were using the computer program? What problems did they have? Which activity did they enjoy the most? (The paper activity or the computer session.) Why? Which activity is easiest to use? Which enabled them to achieve a better presentation? How useful did they find the stamps/motifs? Are they better than using the cut-out pictures of the activity sheets? Why/Why not?

Name _____   Activity 1   Date _____

◆ The house of straw ◆

✦ Colour this picture of the Little Pigs' house of straw.

✦ Colour these pictures. Cut them out and glue them onto the picture above.

ICT Skills
Reception/Year 1

Photocopiable
©Hopscotch Educational Publishing

Name _____   Activity 2   Date _____

◆ The house of sticks ◆

✦ Finish drawing this house of sticks. Colour it in.

✦ Colour these pictures. Cut them out and glue them onto the picture above.

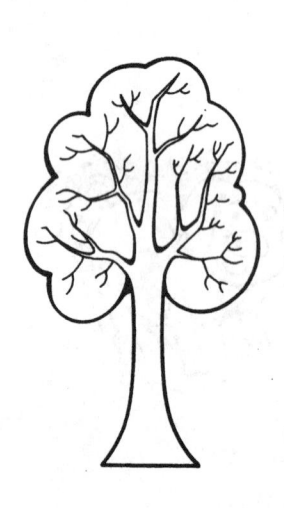

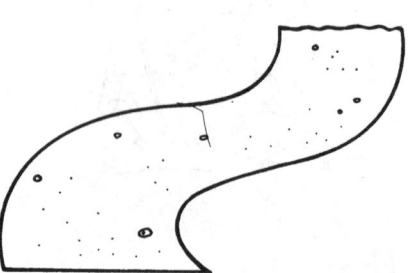

16 ICT Skills
Reception/Year 1

Photocopiable
©Hopscotch Educational Publishing

Name _____ Activity 3   Date _____

◆ The house of bricks ◆

✦ Draw a picture of the Three Little Pigs' house of bricks. Colour it in.

✦ Colour these pictures. Cut them out and glue them onto your picture.

ICT Skills
Reception/Year 1

Photocopiable
©Hopscotch Educational Publishing

17

Lesson 4

Keyboard skills

◆ Learning objectives

- ◆ To recognise, name and identify letters in upper and lower case.
- ◆ To develop familiarity with the keyboard.
- ◆ To select the correct keys from the keyboard for a specific purpose.
- ◆ To use the backspace and caps lock and/or shift keys.
- ◆ To understand that text can be entered into a computer and printed out.

◆ Resources

- ◆ Poster or frieze showing upper and lower case letters or photocopiable page 66.
- ◆ A collection of signs, labels and so on that show different text sizes, colours and fonts.
- ◆ Photocopiable page 65.
- ◆ Aircom CD-Rom Activity 2 and/or a word processor.

◆ Whole class introduction

- ◆ Ask the children to tell you where they can see words and writing in the classroom. What do some of these things tell us? (For example, their names on drawers.) Why do we need signs and labels in our room?
- ◆ Show them the collection of different types of writing. Select two different texts, such as a sign written in capital letters and a coloured book title written in lower case. Can they tell you what is the same and what is different about the writing? Point out any differences in size, colour, font and so on. Can they suggest why the writing may need to be made to look different on different things? Why are words on a sign large, for example?
- ◆ Look at the way some letters are in capitals and some in lower case. Write some of the children's names on the board. Remind them names begin with a capital letter. Look at the letters on an alphabet frieze. Can they find some of these capital letters in the collection of texts?
- ◆ Ask the children what they usually write with – a pencil, a felt-tipped pen? Can they make their own writing different sizes? Can they write in different

colours? Explain that a computer can also be used to do this and that you will be showing them how.

◆ Group activities

Focus group – with the teacher

- ◆ Show the children how to set up the word processor. Set the font very large so they can see what you are presenting on screen. Explain that there are lots of different keys on the keyboard but they are only going to use some of them for the moment. Talk about how the letters are not set out in order like an alphabet and that they may take a long time at first to find the letter they want. (If your keyboard does not have lower case lettering, explain that although the letters on the keyboard are in capitals, they will come out in lower case when they are pressed.)
- ◆ Show the children how to press a key with a light but firm press. Tell them not to hold the key down – show them what happens when you do this. Type a word and teach them how to 'rub it out' using the back space key. Next, explain how to make a capital letter using the caps lock or, more usually, the shift key.
- ◆ Allow each child time to type in their own name. Print them out on separate pieces of paper and invite the children to draw a picture of themselves underneath.

Using the photocopiable activity sheets

- ◆ Use the activity sheets after the computer session.

◆ Plenary session

Discuss any problems the children may have had. Ask them to remind you how to make capital letters. Do they know that the shift key should be held down while pressing the letter key for a single capital and that the caps lock key stays on when pressed? What should they do if they make a mistake? Use page 65 to model the keyboard features.

Name _____ **Activity 1** **Date** _____

✦ The keyboard ✦

✦ Colour in the letters of your name on the keyboard.
   Colour in the ⟵ key.

ICT Skills
Reception/Year 1

Name _____ Activity 2 Date _____

✦ The keyboard ✦

✦ Draw a line from each letter to the correct place on the keyboard. One has been done for you. Colour the ⬅ key in red.

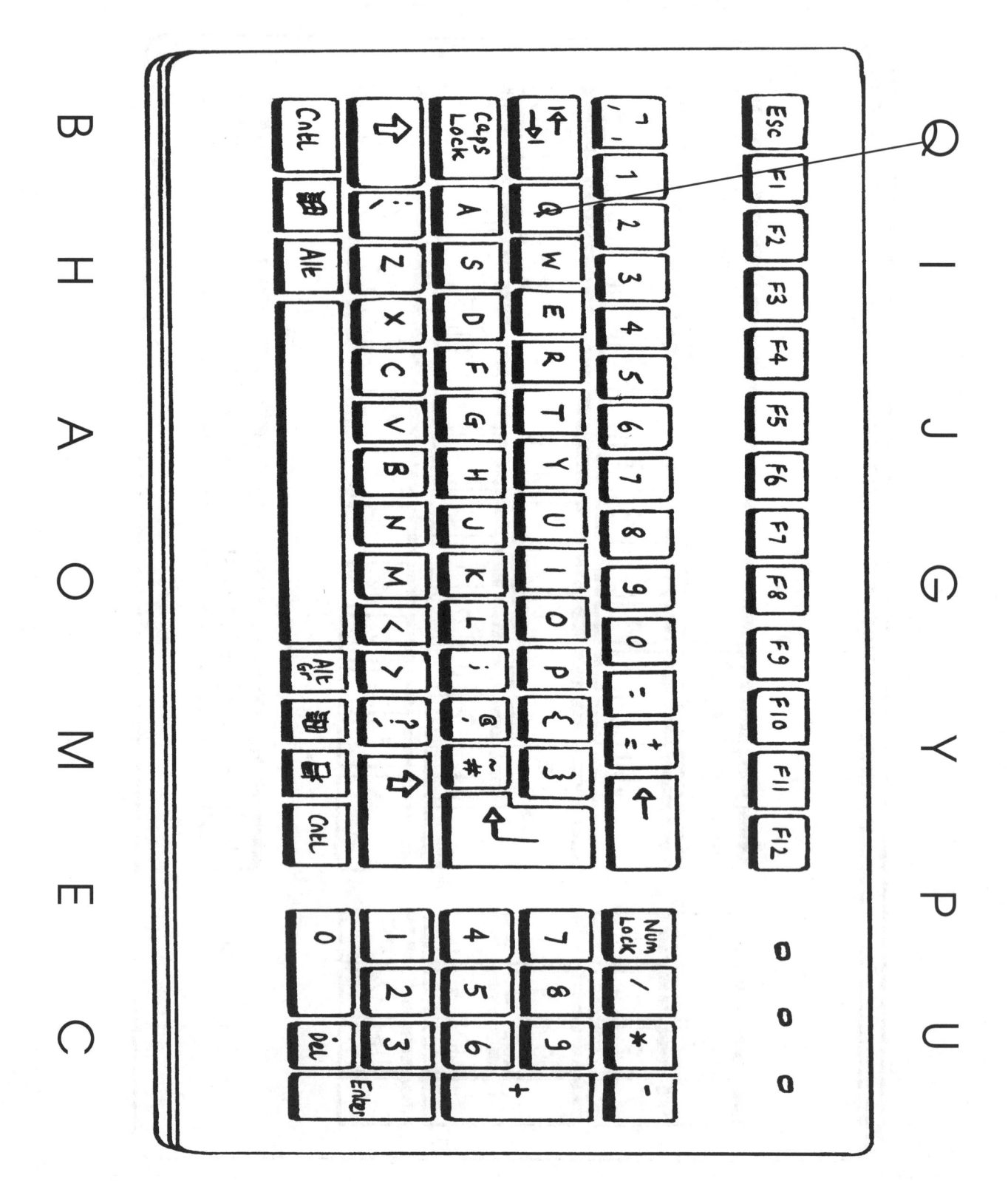

B H A O M E C   I J G Y P U

Name _____ Activity 3 Date _____

✦ The keyboard ✦

✦ Use a keyboard to copy all the missing letters in this picture. Then write in the ⬅ and ⬆ keys.

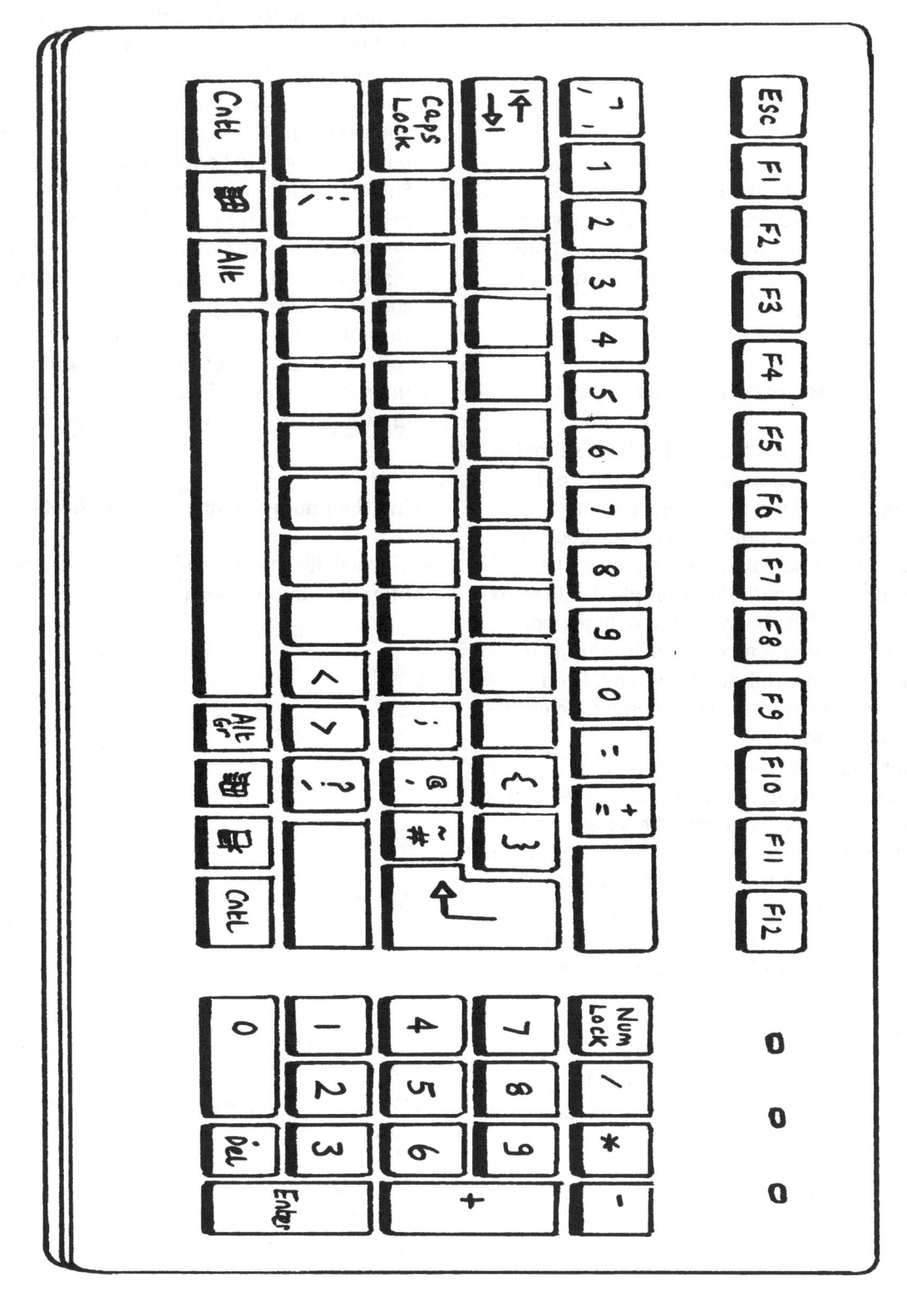

ICT Skills
Reception/Year 1

Photocopiable
©Hopscotch Educational Publishing

21

Lesson 5
Using a word bank

◆ Learning objectives

- To use a word bank to make sentences.
- To be aware that sentences need to make sense.
- To use ICT to assemble text.
- To select and listen to text, using a mouse.

◆ Resources

- A teacher-prepared big book (as in Lesson 2).
- Aircom CD-Rom Activity 3 (a–c) and/or a word processor with a talking word bank facility that enables the children to match the beginning and endings of sentences.

◆ Whole class introduction

- Remind the children about the big book shared in Lesson 2. Share it again to reinforce the words. Tell them that you would like them to make up some sentences about the things in the book. What could they say about the picture of the rubber duck in the bath, for example? Write some of their ideas on the board. Remind them about the need for a capital letter at the beginning of the sentence and a full stop at the end. Read through the sentences together, pointing to each word as you read it.
- Read out one of the sentences again, but this time miss out the last word. Can the children tell you what was wrong? Why doesn't the sentence make sense? Repeat this with other sentences. Then read out a sentence with the words in the wrong order. Ask them to tell you why it doesn't make sense. (The words in the sentences could be written on separate pieces of card so the words can be re-arranged several times to explore making sense further.)
- Tell the children that they are now going to make some sentences themselves using an activity sheet and a computer program. Remind them that their sentences need to make sense.

◆ Group activities

Focus group – with the teacher

- At the computer, remind the children how to hold and move the mouse correctly on the mouse mat. Ask them to tell you which button to click when they want to select something on the screen.
- Show them how to select a word from the word bank and listen to the computer say the word. Show them how to select and listen to each word before choosing it to complete a sentence.
- Read the sentence through together. Does it make sense? Explain the task to the children and make sure they understand what to do.
- Now allow each child an opportunity to make some sentences of their own. Print out and date their work at the end of the session. They could draw a picture to go with their sentence(s).

Using the photocopiable activity sheets

- The activity sheets could be completed before or after the computer session.

◆ Plenary session

Ask someone from each group to share what they did on their activity sheets. Talk about the task done on the computer. Did they find it helpful to hear the computer say the words? Ask the children to remind you what they need to be aware of when making sentences. What are the benefits of using a computer to do this? Is it easier to correct a mistake? What things do they need to remember when using the computer to do this task?

Name _____   Activity 1   Date _____

✦ Making sentences ✦

✦ Choose a word from the box to complete each sentence. Make sure the sentences make sense.

| dog | cup | tap | bed | mat |

The cat is on the _____.

The boy is next to his _____.

This is a big _____.

Water is coming out of the _____.

The dog is on the _____.

✦ On the back of this sheet, write a sentence about something in your house and draw a picture of it.

ICT Skills
Reception/Year 1
©Hopscotch Educational Publishing
23

Name _____   **Activity 2**   Date _____

✦ Making sentences ✦

✦ Choose the correct word from the box so these sentences make sense.

| bird | cat | bowl | sink | table | desk |
| open | shut | bath | dog | book | sock |

The duck is sitting in the _____.

The lamp is on the _____.

The fish is swimming in the _____.

This door is _____.

The boy is playing with the _____.

✦ On the back of this sheet write a sentence about something in your house and draw a picture of it.

Name _____   Activity 3   Date _____

✦ Making sentences ✦

✦ Choose words from the box to write sentences about these pictures. Put in capital letters and full stops. Make sure the sentences make sense.

on	table	are	the	cat	sitting
spoon	a	teapot	is	and	
	asleep	bed	cup		

✦ On the back of this sheet write two sentences about something in your house.

ICT Skills
Reception/Year 1

Photocopiable
©Hopscotch Educational Publishing

25

Lesson 6
Obtaining information

◆ Learning objectives

- To recognise that sounds, pictures and text convey information.
- To identify things that give us information in sound, pictures and text.
- To understand that computers use sound, pictures and text to convey information.
- To know that computers use icons to provice information and instructions.

◆ Resources

- A poster or big book picture of a scene with objects in it that use sound, pictures and text to tell us things, for example a street scene with an ambulance, traffic lights, street signs and picture signs.
- Aircom CD-Rom Activity 4 and/or a multimedia computer program such as a talking book.

◆ Whole class introduction

- Share the large picture with the children. Discuss what is happening in the picture and where it is set. Ask them to tell you the names of some of the things in the picture.
- Ask them to imagine that they are going to visit this place. Can they tell you what sounds they might hear as they walk along? Select some things in the picture that tell us specific information through using sound, such as an ambulance siren. Can they find other things in the picture that make a sound that tells us something? Can they think of other things not in the picture that tell us things by making sounds, such as a whistle or a telephone.
- Repeat this activity using objects that tell us things in pictures and words, like shop signs or picture symbols. Explain that we can learn things everyday by using the sounds, pictures and words around us.
- Finally, tell the children that a computer can also use sounds, pictures and words to tell us things and that they will be using a program that uses all these things.

◆ Group activities

Focus group – with the teacher

- Introduce the program to the children. Show them the icons used in the program and ask them to suggest what information or instruction they might provide. Remind them how to use the mouse correctly to click on the icons to see what happens.
- If applicable, show them how to click on parts of the picture or the text to see what happens. Reinforce this by asking them to predict what might happen if you click on certain things on the next page or screen.
- Tell the children that they do not need to know a great deal more to use the program and that they will learn how to use it as they go along. Encourage them to try things to see what happens. Ask them to see how many different ways the computer program can communicate information to us (words, pictures, sounds, icons).

Using the photocopiable activity sheets

- The activity sheets could be used before or after the computer session.

◆ Plenary session

Ask someone from each group to share what they did on their activity sheet. Does everyone agree with their responses? Discuss the computer program. Did they have any problems? How did they solve them? Ask the children to tell you how they used the program, for example what did they have to do to turn the pages or go to the next screen? How did they make a sound happen? How were they helped to read the words on the screen? Did they enjoy the program? How different is it from watching a television programme or reading a library book, for example? If appropriate, introduce the term 'interactive' here to describe the different responses.

Name _____   Activity 1   Date _____

✦ Sound, pictures and writing ✦

✦ Colour the objects that tell us things when they make a sound.

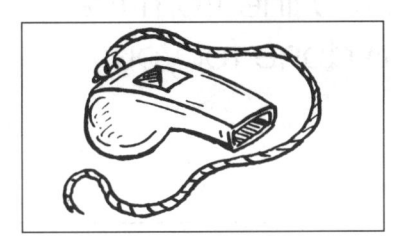

✦ Colour the objects that tell us things in pictures.

✦ Colour the objects that tell us things in writing.

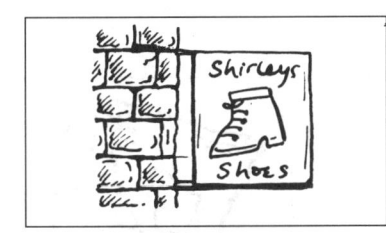

| Name _____ | Activity 2 | Date _____ |

◆ Sound, pictures and writing ◆

◆ Decide whether these objects can tell us things in sound, pictures or writing. Some things can do all three! Draw a line from the object to the correct word(s). One has been done for you.

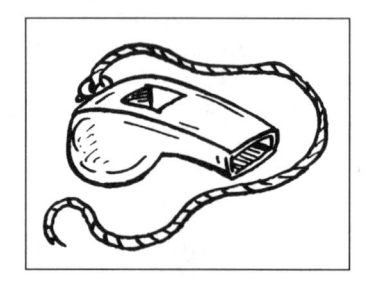

sound

pictures

writing

Name _____   Activity 3   Date _____

✦ Sound, pictures and writing ✦

✦ Complete the table below by deciding whether these objects can tell us things in sound, pictures or writing. The first one has been done for you. Add some more objects of your own.

object	sound	pictures	writing
picture book		✔	✔
television			
road sign			
postcard			
computer			
shop sign			
letter			
newspaper			
a painting			
a poem			
police siren			
whistle			
map of UK			
telephone			

ICT
Reception/Year 1

Photocopiable
©Hopscotch Educational Publishing
29

Lesson 7
Presenting information

◆ Learning objectives

+ To understand that certain 'rules' (or conventions) are applied in communicating and presenting information.
+ To understand that a computer can manipulate the appearance of text for a particular purpose.

◆ Resources

+ A collection of samples of text that are used for different purposes, for example large labels, road signs, newspaper headlines and sub-headings.
+ A prepared set of labels written and stored as files in a word-processor. For example, a label written in a large font with a box around it, a warning sign written in a large red font, a label written in a medium-sized font for a child's drawer and a label written in a coloured, fancy font for a book cover.

◆ Whole class introduction

+ Share the collection of signs and labels. Discuss the purpose of each one and why it might have been produced. Explain that the labels and signs tell us information that we may need to know.
+ Compare the way the signs and labels are presented – look at the difference in font size, style and colour, for example. Why is the writing in a warning sign written in large red lEtters? Why are newspaper headlines larger than the other writing on the page? Why are some signs and labels large and yet others are only small?
+ Explain that some of the conventions used are universal, so that people are aware of what they mean. For example, red is often used to mean danger, symbols on toilet doors are easily recognised as men and women, more important words are often larger in order to gain people's attention, and so on.

◆ Group activities

Focus group – with the teacher

+ Show the children the prepared files on the word-processor. For each one, ask them what they think the label might be used for. Discuss the size, style and colour of the text and why it has been be presented in that way.
+ Discuss any borders that have been used and how these help to attract attention.
+ Show the children how the computer can be used to change the appearance of the text by changing the font size, style and colour of one of the examples. How might the changes affect what the sign/label is used for and where it might be used? (For example, a large warning sign might be used as a poster and a small warning sign might be used as a label on a piece of equipment.)
+ Discuss the possibilities of using a computer to make signs and labels. What are the advantages of using the computer over pencil and paper methods?

Using the photocopiable activity sheets

+ The activity sheets could be used before or after the computer session.

◆ Plenary session

Share the responses to the activity sheets. What decisions did the children have to make? Did everyone colour the stop/danger signs in red? Have they used green for go? What considerations needed to be made in deciding how to write the name labels? Should the writing on the drawer label be larger than for a ruler or a name badge? Why/why not? Is the person's last name as necessary as the first name? Is colour important on name labels? Does colour affect the ease of reading the label? Do some colours stand out more than others? Could the computer be useful for making name labels? Why/why not?

Name _____   Activity 1   Date _____

✦ Signs and labels ✦

✦ Colour these signs and labels.

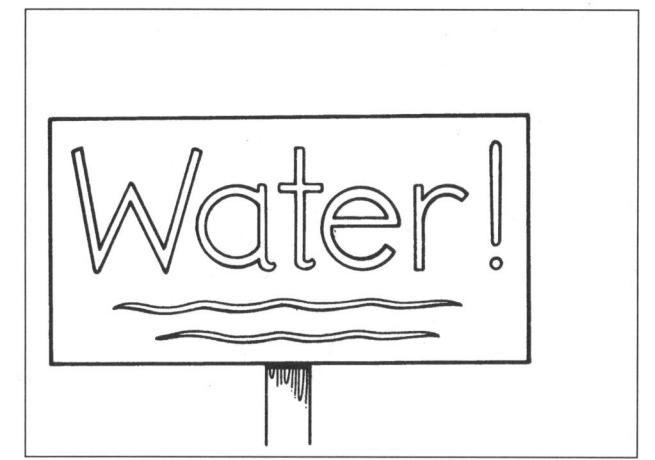

[STOP] [Water!]

[30] [GO]

✦ Write and colour a name badge for yourself.

ICT
Reception/Year 1

ICT Skills

Photocopiable
©Hopscotch Educational Publishing

Name _____ Activity 2 Date _____

✦ Signs and labels ✦

✦ Draw a STOP sign and a GO sign in the boxes below. Colour them in the colours you think they should be.

✦ Write and colour two name labels for yourself. One is to go on your drawer front and the other to be worn as a badge.

drawer label

name badge

Name _____   Activity 3   Date _____

✦ Signs and labels ✦

✦ Draw and colour these signs in the boxes below.

    1   DANGER   2   Mind the step
    3   GO   4   Flood

✦ In the box below, write and colour two name labels for yourself, one to go on a ruler and one to wear as a badge. Decide on the colour and size of writing to use.

ICT
Reception/Year 1

Lesson 8

Sorting

◆ Learning objectives

- ✦ To describe objects using key words.
- ✦ To sort objects using different criteria.
- ✦ To use a word bank to present information.

◆ Resources

- ✦ A collection of household objects specific to certain rooms, such as the kitchen and bathroom, some of which are the same colour.
- ✦ Labels for size, colour and shape.
- ✦ Photocopiable page 67 as a further activity (see page 62).
- ✦ Aircom CD-Rom Activity 5 (a–c) and/or a word processor with a word bank and graphic insert capability.

◆ Whole class introduction

- ✦ Sit the children in a circle. Tell them that you are going to show them some things that can be found inside a home. Place each object, one at a time in the centre of the circle. For each object say what it is and ask the children questions about it, such as: 'What colour is it?' 'What shape is it?' 'Is it bigger or smaller than…(one of the other objects)?' When all the objects are in the circle, remind the children of all the information they gave you about some of the objects. Use the word 'information' as you tell them.
- ✦ Now tell them that you are going to describe an object and they have to guess which one it is. As you describe it, hold up a label for each word you use, for example 'long', 'blue' (toothbrush). Ask a child to say or point to the object they think it is. Check to see if this is correct by reading out and placing the labels in front of the object. Say 'long, blue toothbrush'. Repeat this for several objects before asking some children to take turns leading the game.
- ✦ Tell the children you are now going to do something different. This time you are going to pick out some of the objects and sort them into two groups. Can they work out how you have sorted them? For example, all blue things in one group and white things in another. Continue the game, sorting in different ways, letting the children take turns in sorting and explaining how they are sorted.
- ✦ Explain that they will now do some more sorting of their own, using an activity sheet and a computer program.

◆ Group activities

Focus group – with the teacher

- ✦ Prepare a word bank containing the names, shapes, sizes and colours of some common household objects.
- ✦ Show the children how to use the mouse to select the appropriate name, size, shape and colour from the word bank to describe each object. Give them the opportunity to do this by themselves and, if possible, print out their work.
- ✦ Using the Aircom CD-Rom, show the children how to use the mouse to select an object and drag it to the appropriate place. Tell them that once they have completed the activity they will have to sort the same objects in a different way, just like they did with the objects in the class session. Completed activities can be printed out and retained as a progress record.

Using the photocopiable activity sheets

- ✦ The activity sheets could be used before or after the computer session.

◆ Plenary session

Share the responses to the activity sheets and discuss any problems the children may have had. Ask them to explain the computer task and show any printed work. Use the word 'information' when sharing the work and emphasise how much information the children found out about their objects.

Name _____ Activity 1 Date _____

◆ Sorting ◆

◆ Circle the object that is long and white.

◆ Circle the object that is big and round.

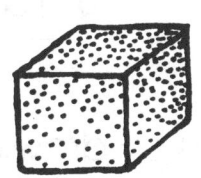

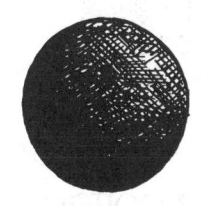

◆ Colour all the bathroom things in RED.
  Colour all the kitchen things in BLUE.

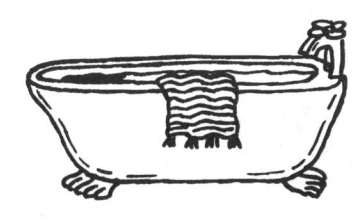

ICT Skills
Reception/Year 1

35

©Hopscotch Educational Publishing

Name _____   Activity 2   Date _____

✦ Sorting ✦

✦ Label the objects by drawing a line from each one to the correct label(s).

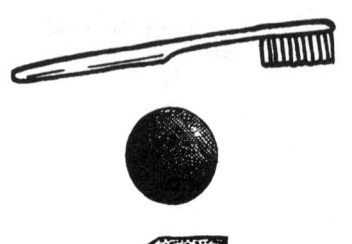

white		black
thin		fat
round	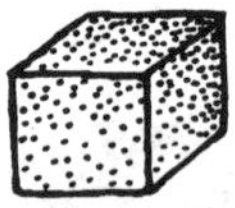	square

✦ Sort these objects into kitchen or bathroom things by drawing a line from the object to the correct room.

ICT Skills
Reception/Year 1

Photocopiable
©Hopscotch Educational Publishing

Name _____ Activity 3 Date _____

✦ Sorting ✦

✦ Complete the table for each object. The first one has been done for you.

object	black	white	round	square	long	short
comb	✔				✔	
cube						
ball						
toothbrush						

✦ Sort these objects into the correct room by drawing a line from each object to a room.

kitchen

bathroom

bedroom

ICT Skills
Reception/Year 1

Photocopiable
©Hopscotch Educational Publishing

37

Lesson 9

Pictograms

Learning objectives

- To understand that data can be collected and presented in a pictogram.
- To use pictograms to answer simple questions.
- To understand that ICT can be used to create pictograms.

Resources

- Magazine pictures of the following foods: spaghetti, hamburger, beans on toast, rice dish, roast chicken and a salad.
- Photocopiable page 68.
- Aircom CD-Rom Activity 6 and/or a graphing package that creates pictograms.

Whole class introduction

- Ask the children to imagine that you are going to cook them a special meal today. Show them the magazine pictures of all the foods they can choose from. (You may want to present this as a big book menu.) Talk about each food and whether or not they have eaten it before. Tell them which one is your favourite.
- Ask them to choose just one of the foods that they would like to eat. 'Serve' each child their choice by giving them a cut out picture of their meal from photocopiable page 68.
- Ask them how they could find out how many of each meal you would have to serve. Line the children up into their meal groups and count the number of children in each line. Explain that they could do this in a different way to make a class record. Ask each child in turn to bring you their food picture and glue them onto a large piece of paper attached to the wall to make a pictogram. Ask them all to count the number of pictures in each food group – is it the same as the number counted when they were in lines?
- Explain how the pictures represent one person's choice of food. Then ask them simple questions relating to the pictogram, such as: 'How many people in the class want a hamburger meal?'

'Which meal did only (2, 3, 4 and so on) people want?' 'Which meal did most people want?'
- Tell the children that they will now do some more work using pictograms on an activity sheet as well as a computer program.

Group activities

Focus group – with the teacher

- Tell the children that a computer can also be used to make a pictogram just like the one they made earlier on the wall chart.
- Show them how to select appropriate icons to represent their data in the computer program.
- Allow each child time to input their choice. Print out the pictogram after all the children have entered their data.

Using the photocopiable activity sheets

- The activity sheets could be used before or after the computer session. Explain the tasks on the sheets very carefully before the children begin.

Plenary session

Share the responses to the activity sheets – does everyone agree? Share the printed pictogram of the children's own data input. Ask simple questions relating to it. Discuss any problems the children may have had in completing the sheets or the computer program. Provide each child with a copy of the printed pictogram and ask them all to write a sentence (or scribe it for them) about it underneath.

Name _____   Activity 1   Date _____

✦ Favourite foods ✦

✦ This is a pictogram of the favourite lunches of some children at Redhill Primary School. Colour it in.

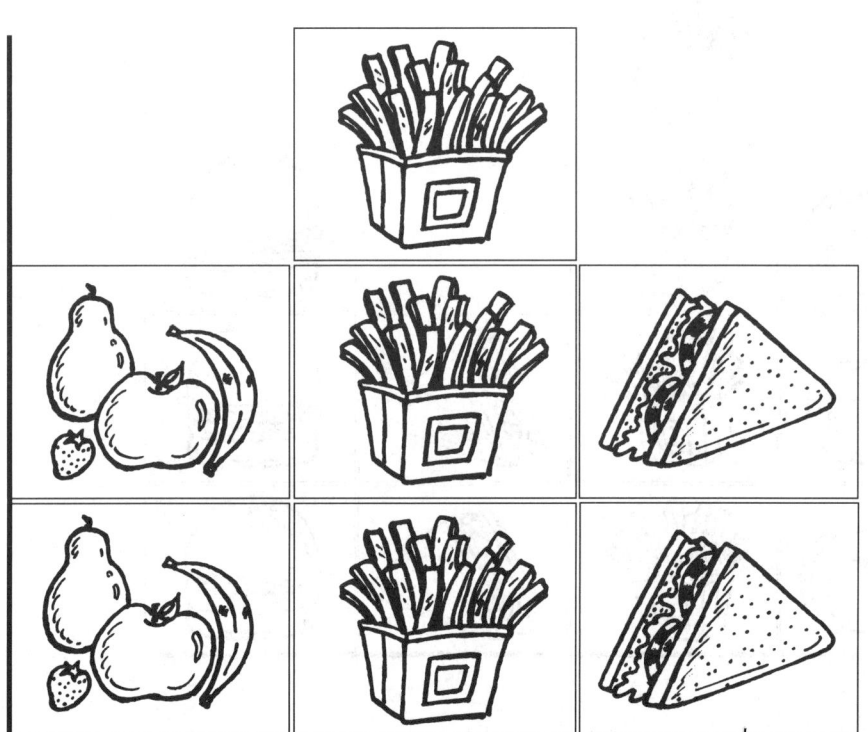

✦ Circle the correct answer.

How many children like 🍎   ?   1   2   3

How many children like 🍟   ?   1   2   3

How many children like 🥪   ?   1   2   3

✦ On the back of this sheet draw a picture of your favourite lunch.

ICT Skills
Reception/Year 1

Name _____ Activity 2 Date _____

✦ Favourite foods ✦

✦ This is a pictogram of the favourite lunches of some children from Redhill Primary School. Colour it in.

✦ Answer these questions.

How many children like 🍎 ? ☐

How many children like 🍟 ? ☐

How many children like 🥪 ? ☐

How many children like 🍔 ? ☐

✦ On the back of this sheet draw a picture of your favourite lunch.

Name _____   Activity 3   Date _____

✦ Favourite foods ✦

✦ This is a pictogram of the favourite lunches of some children from Redhill Primary School. Colour it in.

✦ Answer these questions.

How many children like 🍟 ? ☐

How many children like 🍛 ? ☐

How many children like 🍎 ? ☐

How many children like 🍔 ? ☐

How many children like 🥪 ? ☐

Which lunch is the most favourite? _____

Which lunch is the least favourite? _____

ICT Skills
Reception/Year 1

Photocopiable
©Hopscotch Educational Publishing

41

Lesson 10
Controlling machines & devices

◆ Learning objectives

- To understand that machines and devices must be controlled to work.
- To sort things into those that can be controlled and those that cannot.
- To recognise and use signs and symbols for control.
- To use on/off switches and control buttons.
- To use a tape recorder to record sounds.

◆ Resources

- Magazine pictures of household objects, some of which can be controlled (television, microwave, washing machine) and some that cannot (sofa, desk, mat).
- A collection of things with on/off switches, such as a calculator, battery-operated toy, lamp and torch.
- Photocopiable page 69.
- Tape recorders.
- Aircom CD-Rom Activity 7.

◆ Whole class introduction

- Show the children some pictures of things they might find in a house. Ask them to tell you what each object is. Talk about how, in order to use some things in the home, we need to turn them on and press some buttons or turn some dials. Which things in the pictures would they have to turn on or use buttons to make them work? Sort the pictures into two groups – controlled machines and devices and non-controlled ones.
- Hold up a battery-operated toy. Turn it on. Ask the children 'Is this toy alive? What makes it move?' Explain that the toy needs a battery to make it work and a switch to turn the energy from the battery on and off. Talk about how machines in the home use mains electricity instead of batteries to make them work and that some of these machines have switches and some need to be turned on and off at the mains.
- Discuss why it is important to have on/off switches. Discuss safety issues, such as what might happen if a cooker could not be turned up or down or on and off. Explain that this is why it is so important to be able to control these devices.
- Show the other items with on/off switches. Can the children think of other items with switches?

◆ Group activities

Focus group – with the teacher

- The following could be carried out with the whole class together or within small groups.
- Show the children a tape recorder. Remind them that in order for it to work it needs to be switched on. (If it is a mains recorder, discuss safety issues such as how to hold and place the plug correctly into the socket.) Switch it on. Pretend you are confused because nothing has happened yet – what else would you have to do to make it work? Talk about how you need to press buttons in order to control the machine.
- Use the cards on page 69 to explain the symbols and what they mean. Where else have the children seen these symbols? Why is it important to have the same symbols on different machines?
- Demonstrate how to use the recorder to tape your voice. Discuss the correct order in which to press the buttons both for recording and playback. Remind the children to check that the tape is fully rewound before they begin. Divide the children into groups and ask them to record some sounds.
- Activity 7 on the Aircom CD-Rom can be used as an independent task. It allows the children to interact with household objects that can be switched on and off and be controlled.

Using the photocopiable activity sheets

- Use the sheets to reinforce the lesson.

◆ Plenary session

Discuss the recording task. Did the children have any problems? Listen to some recordings. Agree on the steps needed to make a recording. Ask them to tell you how to rewind the tape. Share the responses to the activity sheets.

Name _____   Activity 1   Date _____

✦ Making it work ✦

✦ Colour all the things that have an on/off switch.

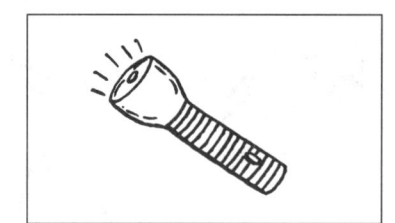

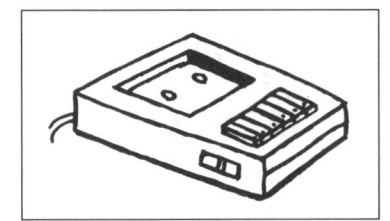

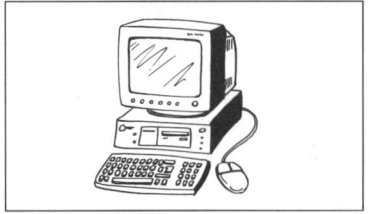

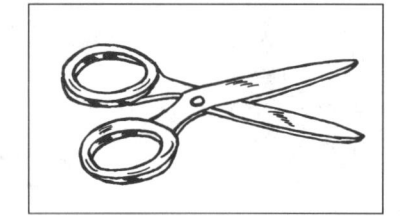

✦ Label the buttons on this tape recorder by drawing a line from the label to the correct place.

stop

on/off

record

play

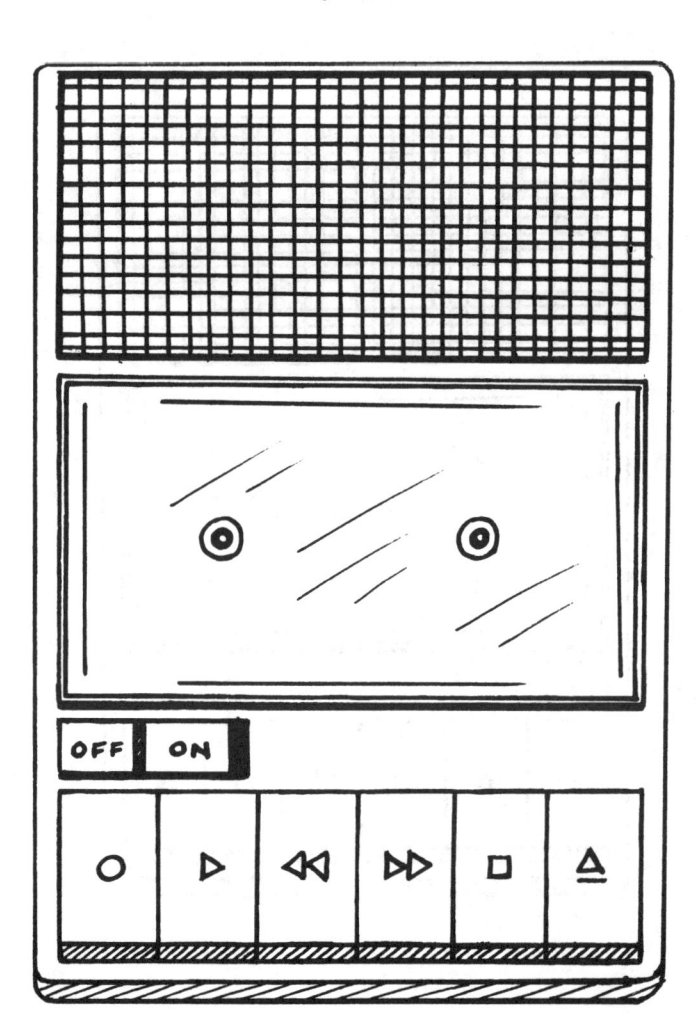

ICT Skills
Reception/Year 1

43

©Hopscotch Educational Publishing

Name _____   Activity 2   Date _____

✦ Making it work ✦

✦ Put a ✔ next to all the things that have an on/off switch.

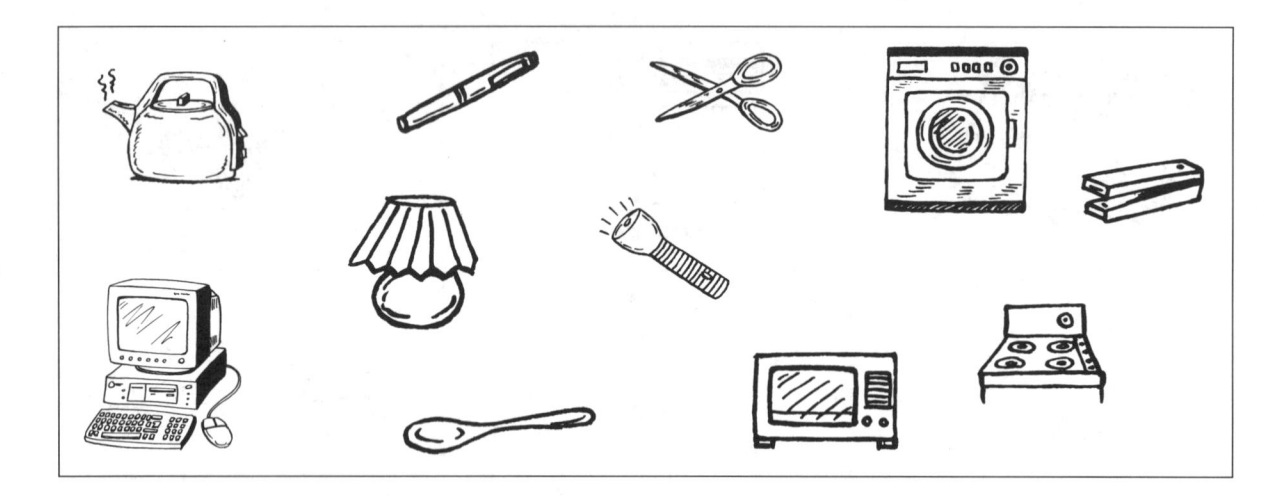

✦ Label the buttons on this tape recorder by drawing a line from the label to the correct place.

stop

record

fast forward

play

on/off

rewind

ICT Skills
Reception/Year 1

Photocopiable
©Hopscotch Educational Publishing

Name _____ Activity 3 Date _____

✦ Making it work ✦

✦ Complete this table by putting a ✔ next to all objects that have an on/off switch.

object	on/off switch?	object	on/off switch?
computer		microwave	
book		tin opener	
scissors		dishwasher	
kettle		cooker	
video		pen	
torch		hi-fi	

✦ Write the names of the buttons on this tape recorder. Use a dictionary to help you.

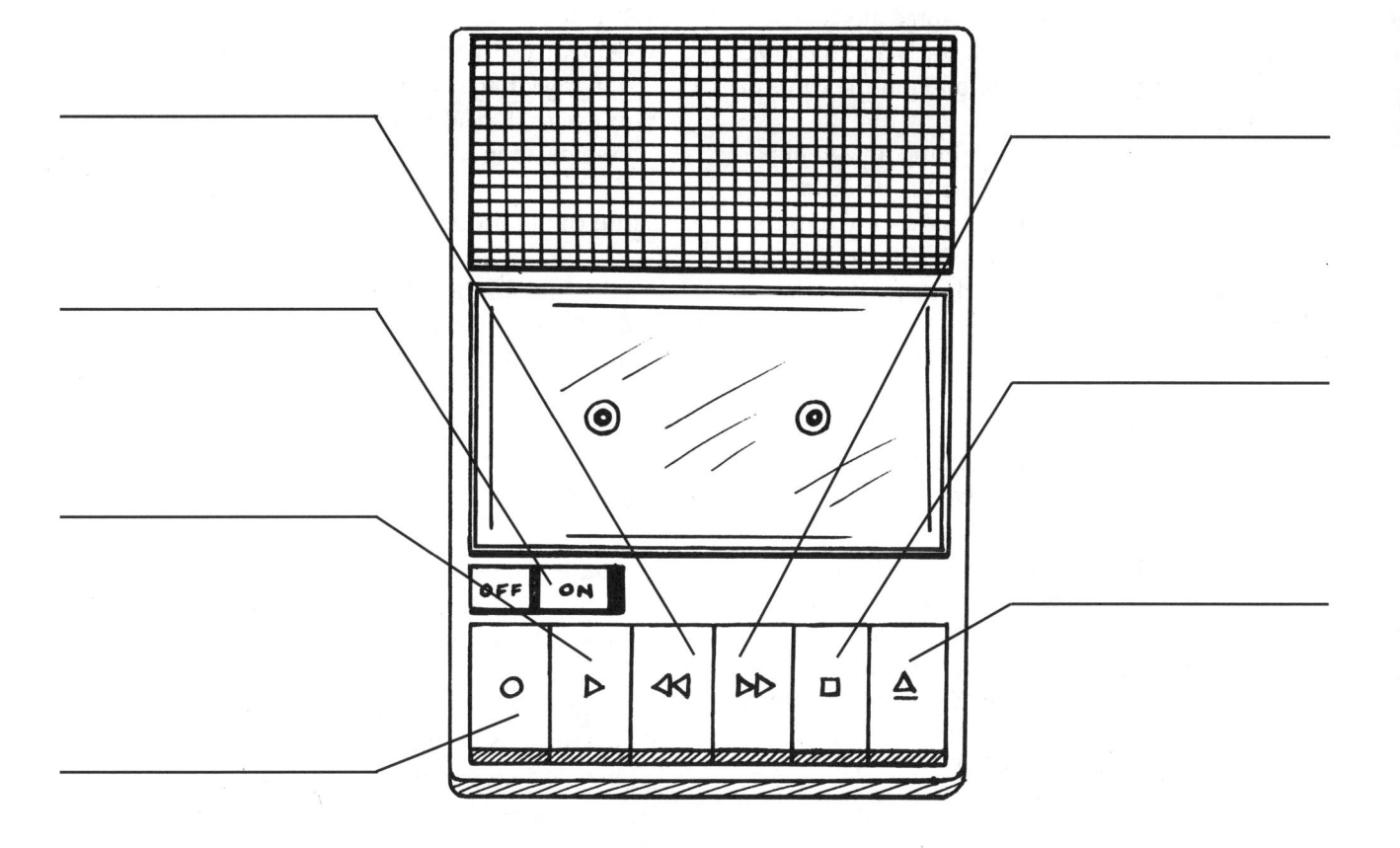

Lesson 11
Sequencing instructions

◆ Learning objectives

- To understand that machines and devices can be controlled by a sequence of actions.
- To understand that sequencing affects outcome.
- To put instructions in the correct sequence to achieve the correct results.

◆ Resources

- Pop-up toaster and some bread.
- Tape recorders.
- Photocopiable page 70, cut out and mounted on to card.
- Aircom CD-Rom Activity 8 (a–d).

◆ Whole class introduction

- Show the toaster to the children. Ask them to imagine that they have been asked to explain to someone else how to make some toast. Do they think this would be easy to do? What do they think would be the first task? Agree this together and show them the mounted cards from page 70. Agree each of the next steps and put the cards on display in order.
- Try out the steps by demonstrating how to make some toast. (Use the time while the bread is cooking to talk about safety issues – not to put anything other than bread inside the toaster, how to hold the plug correctly and so on.) Was the order correct?
- Re-arrange the pictures – is it still possible to make the toast using this sequence? Explain that it is sometimes very important to get the steps in the right order when doing things or else something may go wrong. Liken this to a recipe. Is it important to follow a recipe in the right order? What might happen if you did not? Is it always necessary to do this when cooking? Does it matter if we put the cream or jam on first when adding toppings to a scone, for example?
- Talk about other times when it is important to do things in the correct order, such as using a telephone or making a model.

- Tell the children they are now going to think about the correct order for doing things when using a tape recorder.

◆ Group activities

Focus group – with the teacher.

- This discussion could be carried out with the whole class or within small groups.
- Show the tape recorder to the children. Remind them of the activities they did in Lesson 10. Do they think that it is important to do things in the right order when using a tape recorder? What might happen if they did not?
- Show them a tape that is re-wound. Ask them to tell you what they think the right steps might be to tell someone how to play the tape using the recorder. What would they need to do (or check) first? Agree each step and write the instructions on the board. Then follow the instructions to play the tape. Are the steps correct? Make any necessary alterations and agree on the final order.
- The activity on the Aircom CD-Rom contains two sequencing tasks – putting a story into sequence and repeating a sequence of given shapes. It is aimed at three different ability levels and can be used as an independent task.

Using the photocopiable activity sheets

- The children should complete the activity sheet after the focus group session. Provide them with a tape recorder.

◆ Plenary session

Share and agree the responses to the activity sheets. Can the order be different and still work? What would happen, for example, if the recorder was not switched on first? The children could be challenged to write and/or draw instructions of their own for demonstrating how to record onto tape.

Name _____   **Activity 1**   **Date** _____

✦ Put them in order ✦

✦ Cut out each picture. Put them in the right order to show how to rewind a tape.

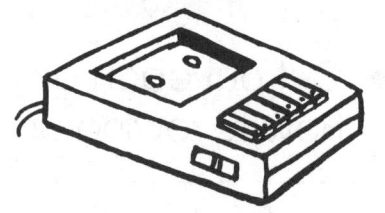

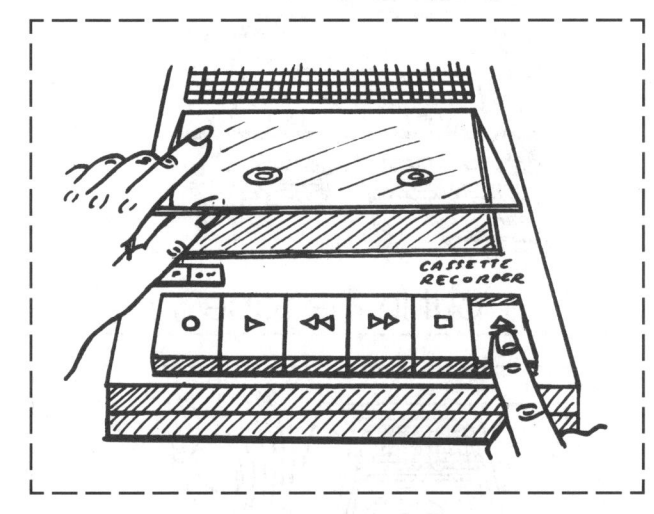

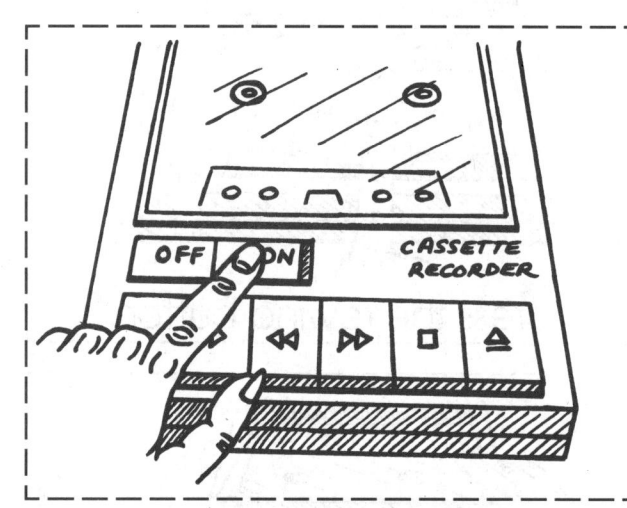

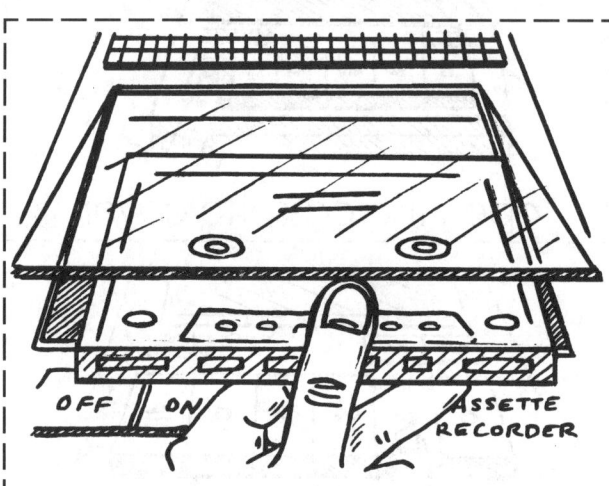

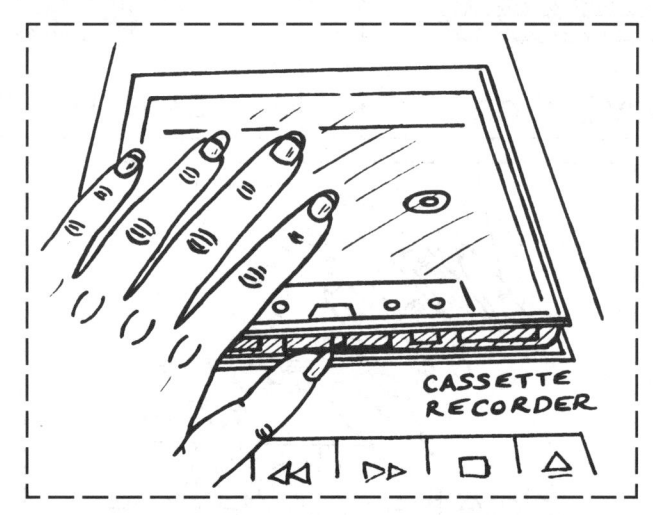

ICT Skills
Reception/Year 1

47

©Hopscotch Educational Publishing

Name _____   Activity 2   Date _____

✦ Put them in order ✦

✦ Cut out each box below. Put them in the right order to show how to rewind and play a tape.

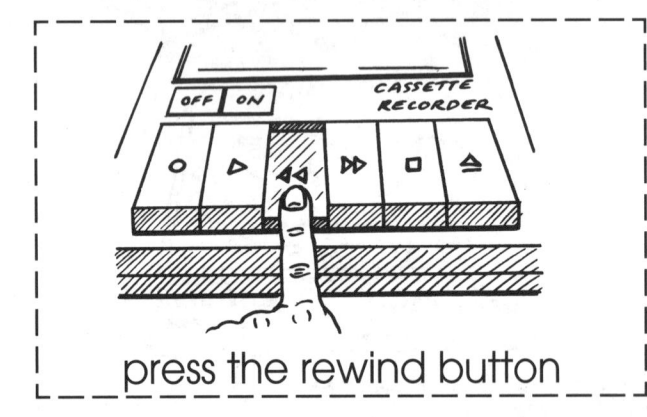

press the rewind button	put in the tape
open the cassette cover	listen to the tape
press the play button	switch on the recorder

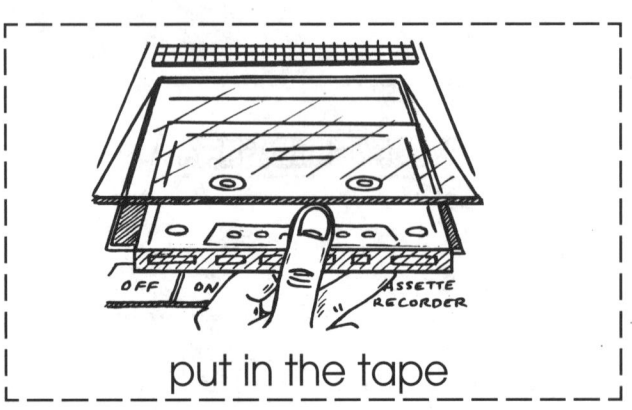

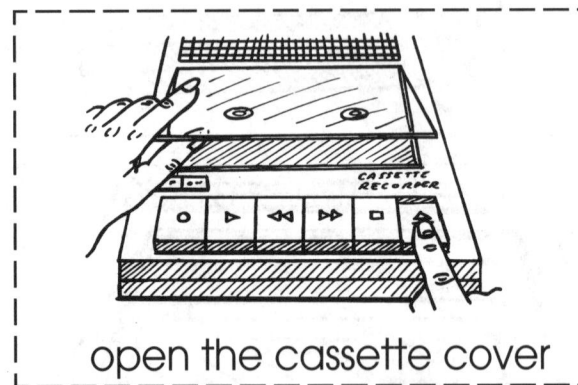

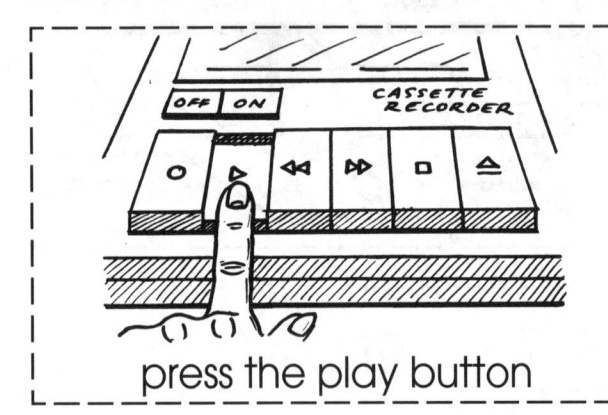

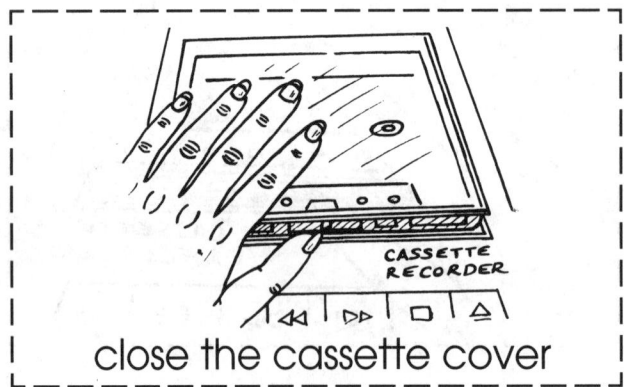

close the cassette cover

ICT Skills
Reception/Year 1

Photocopiable
©Hopscotch Educational Publishing

Name _____ Activity 3 Date _____

✦ Put them in order ✦

✦ Cut out each box below. Put them in the right order to show how to rewind and play a tape and then stop it. Two of the steps are missing. Decide what they are, then draw and write the instructions in the two empty boxes.

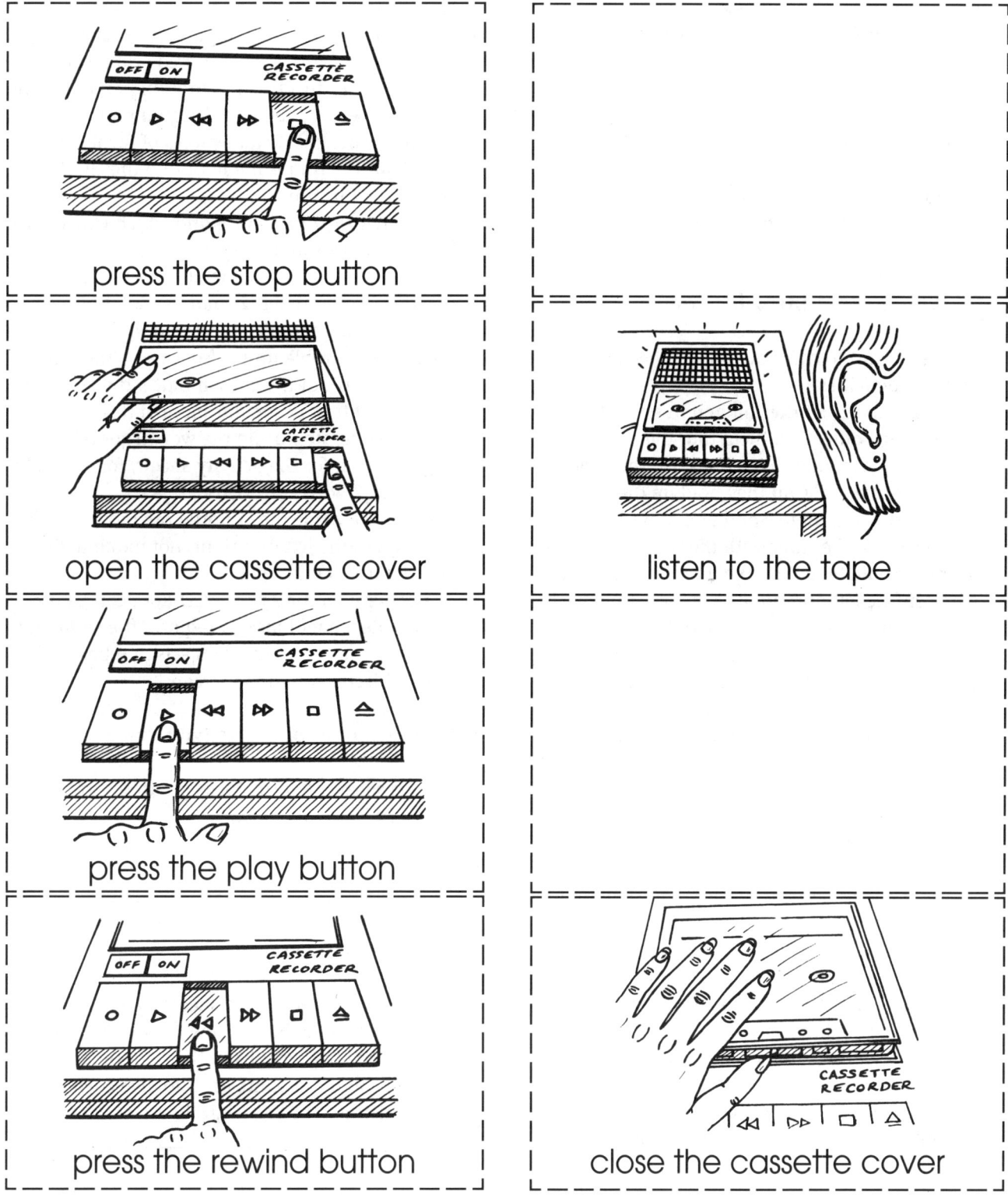

press the stop button

open the cassette cover

listen to the tape

press the play button

press the rewind button

close the cassette cover

ICT Skills
Reception/Year 1

Photocopiable
©Hopscotch Educational Publishing

49

Lesson 12
Following instructions

♦ Learning objectives

♦ To understand that instructions can be given in a common language.
♦ To know that instructions can include measurable units in a common language.
♦ To follow simple, measurable directional instructions.

♦ Resources

♦ A large open space.
♦ Aircom CD-Rom Activity 9 (a–f).

♦ Whole class introduction

♦ You may want to carry out several lessons based on these activities.
1. In a large space, sit the children in several rows behind each other. Tell them that they are going to learn how to follow directions. Do they know what 'left' means? Can they hold up their left hand? Ask them all to stand and move sideways to the left. Do the same with the right. (A red spot for right could be put on the hands of children who confuse left and right.) Ask them to move to short sequences after listening to the instructions first, for example 'Move right, then left. Go.' (If you use the term 'go' this will prepare the children for later activities using a floor robot.)
2. Repeat the above for 'forward' and 'backward'.
3. Repeat this using all four terms. The children will probably bump into each other. Use this problem to introduce the idea of units of measurement, such as steps. (Move two steps forward, then two steps left. Go.) Discuss how even using steps may cause problems because one person's step might be larger or smaller than another's. Can they suggest ways of overcoming this? Discuss the importance of standardising the units used and using the same words to give the directions.
4. Divide the class into small groups and ask them to give each other simple directions to negotiate an obstacle or to get to a certain place. Discuss how the position of a person (which way they are facing) will affect the instructions given.

♦ Group activities

Focus group – with the teacher

♦ This activity can be carried out with the whole class or within small groups.
♦ Teach the children how to play the 'design a room' game. Mark out a squared grid outside using chalk or inside using masking tape. Tell the children they are going to design a room by deciding where particular pieces of furniture might go. The grid is the floor and the children will be the furniture.
♦ Agree on a starting square and which way to face then give very simple instructions to an individual or pair to follow, such as 'Start, forward 2 squares, left 2 squares. Go'. Make sure that the children understand that in this case, the agreed measurable unit is 'squares'. When the children arrive at the chosen place, they can hold a picture of that particular piece of furniture. After a while, stop using the word 'square' to prepare them for the activity sheets, for example 'Start, left 2, forward 1. Go').
Note: at this stage the children are moving sideways to the left and right, not making 90 degree turns on the spot.
♦ The activity on the Aircom CD-Rom can be used as an independent task. It requires the children to follow instructions to find objects in a box and to move objects around the screen.

Using the photocopiable activity sheets

♦ Use the sheets after the focus group session. (Forward is up the page.)

♦ Plenary session

Share the responses to the sheets. What problems did they have? How important was it to follow the instructions in the right order? The children could use blank grids to give each other verbal instructions to design their own rooms.

Name _____ Activity 1 Date _____

✦ Design a room ✦

✦ Cut out the pictures at the bottom of the page. Follow the instructions to put the things in each room. Glue them in place. Colour them in.

Bedroom

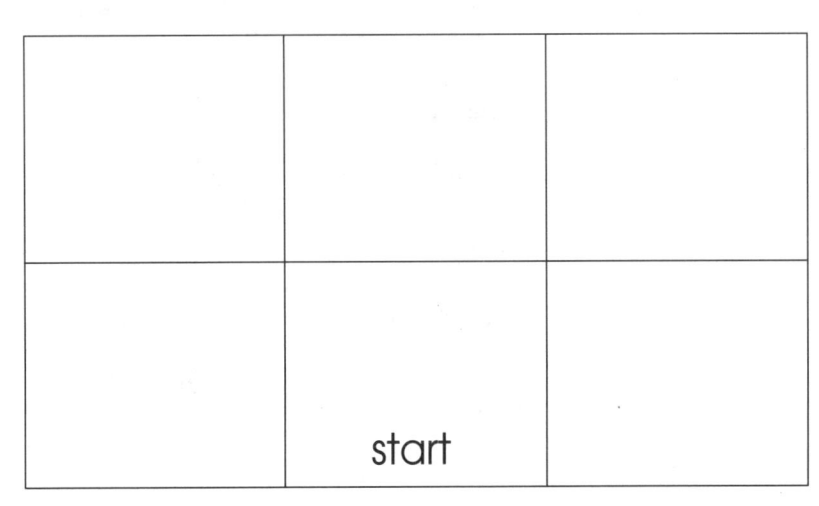

	start	

bed 
start
right 1
forward 1

Bathroom

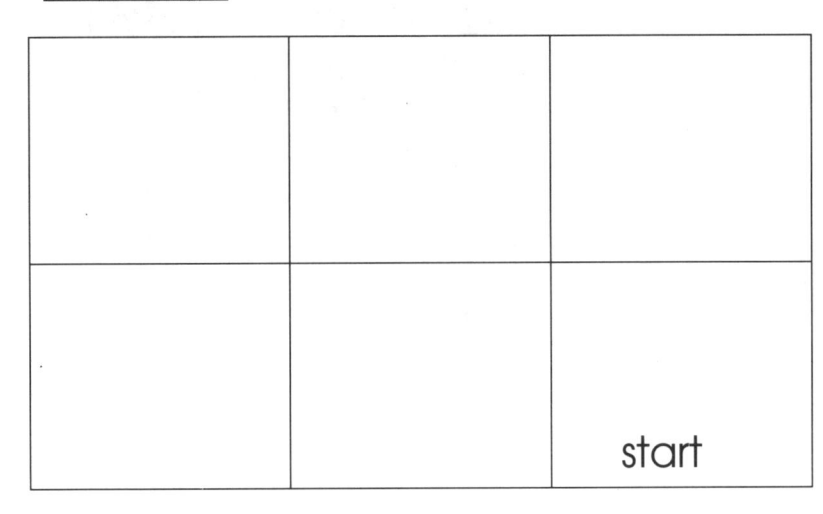

		start

sink 
start
forward 1
left 1

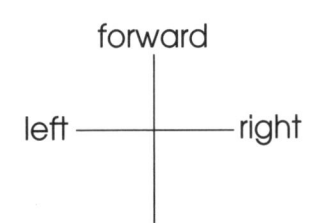

forward
left —— right

ICT Skills
Reception/Year 1

51

Name _____   Activity 2   Date _____

◆ Design a room ◆

◆ Cut out the pictures at the bottom of the page. Follow the instructions to put the things in each room. Glue them in place. Colour them in.

Bedroom

	start	

desk
start
left 1
forward 1

bed
start
right 1
forward 1
left 1

Bathroom

	start	

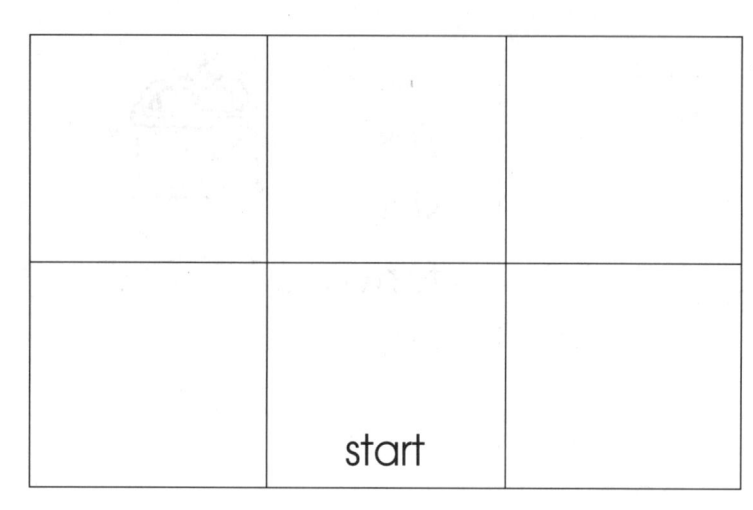

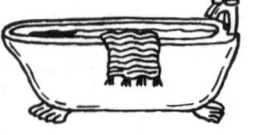

bath
start
forward 1
right 1

sink
start
right 1
forward 1
left 2

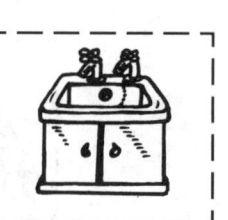

Name _____   Activity 3   Date _____

✦ Design a room ✦

✦ Cut out the pictures at the bottom of the page. Follow the instructions to put the things in each room. Glue them in place. Colour them in. Write the instructions for the table.

Living room

television 
start
forward 3
right 2
backward 1

book case 
start
right 2
forward 3
left 2

chair 
start
right 1
forward 3
right 1
backward 2

table
start

ICT Skills
Reception/Year 1

Photocopiable
©Hopscotch Educational Publishing

53

Lesson 13

Recording instructions

◆ Learning objectives

- ◆ To understand that instructions can be recorded.
- ◆ To record a sequence of instructions in a common format.
- ◆ To write own instructions.
- ◆ To understand that symbols can be used to abbreviate instructions.

◆ Resources

- ◆ Large open space with grid marked out as in Lesson 10.
- ◆ Photocopiable page 71.
- ◆ Aircom CD-Rom Activity 10 (a–c).

◆ Whole class activities

- ◆ Remind the children about the 'design a room' activities previously carried out. Tell them that they are going to continue with this idea today. Ask a child to stand in a square to represent a piece of furniture, such as a table. Agree a start square and which way to face. Pair up the other children (perhaps a more able writer with a less able one). Tell them to imagine they have to program a special housework robot to go and dust the table. Ask them to write down the instructions for the robot to get from the start square to the table. Let them decide how they want to record their instructions.
- ◆ When they have completed their task, ask everyone to sit down to watch while one pair reads out their instructions to a chosen 'robot' to follow. Does the robot understand the instructions? Does he/she reach the table successfully? Do other pairs have different instructions but still end up at the same place?
- ◆ Discuss how the children recorded their instructions – share the different approaches. Has anyone used abbreviations/drawings/symbols? What words were commonly used? Discuss possible ideas for making their instructions simpler and shorter.
- ◆ Tell them that if we were to program the robot by pressing buttons, we could use symbols and numbers to give the instructions. Show them the symbol cards on page 71 and explain what they mean. Introduce the term 'repeat' and ensure they understand its meaning. Make up very simple sequences for them to follow using the symbol cards, such as the one below.

↑ 2   ↱ 1   (forward 2, right 1)

- ◆ Place the cards where all the children can see them easily. Continue using the cards (and saying the words at the same time) to direct pairs of children to different places on the grid.
Note: you could introduce another symbol for 'go' to prepare the children for programming a floor robot. 'Go' comes at the end of the sequence.
- ◆ Ask the children to rewrite their original instructions using the new symbols.
- ◆ The activity on the Aircom CD-Rom can be used as an independent task to support the lesson and prepare the children for using a floor robot. Show them how to use the 'control pad' and how the instructions are recorded and can be replayed.

◆ Group activities

Using the photocopiable activity sheets

- ◆ The activity sheets should be used after the whole class activities.

◆ Plenary session

Share the responses to the activity sheets. Discuss the fact that different sequences can be used and still be correct. How many different ways can the robot move from start to the sink on sheet 2, for example? Do they think symbols are easier to follow and write than whole words each time?

Name _____   Activity 1   Date _____

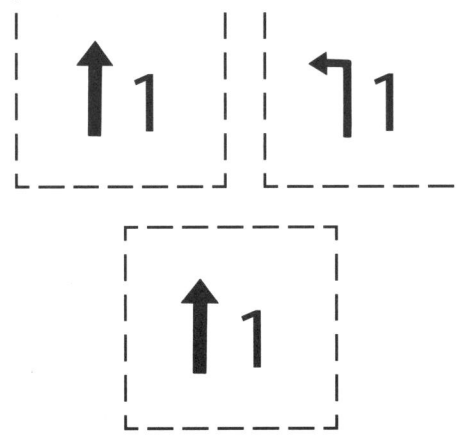

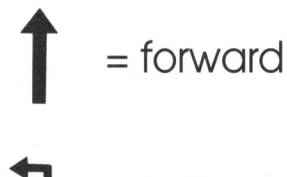

✦ Robby Robot ✦

✦ Help Robby Robot make the bed by cutting out the cards and putting them in the right order to tell him how to get from start to the bed.

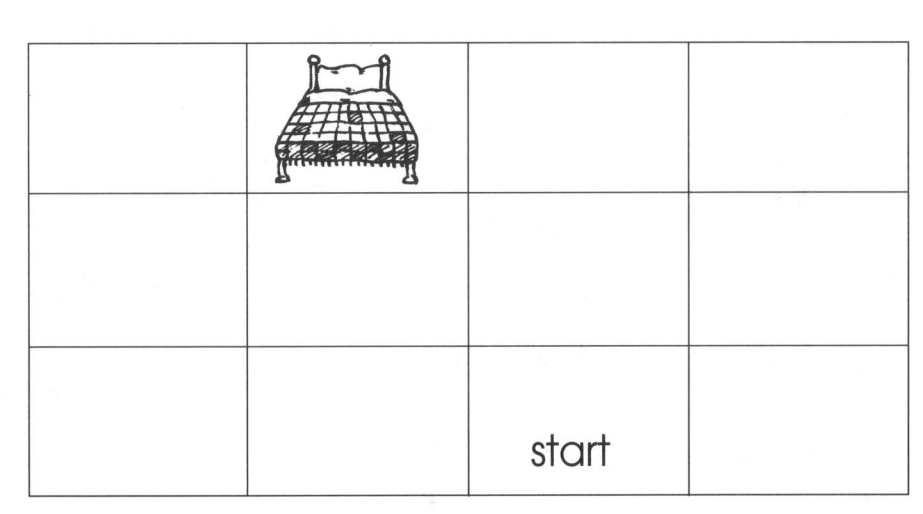

	🛏		
		start	

✦ Stick the cards in the right order here.

↑1   ↰1

↑1

↑ = forward

↰ = left

ICT Skills
Reception/Year 1

55

Name _____ Activity 2 Date _____

✦ Robby Robot ✦

✦ Help Robby Robot to clean the kitchen by writing the instructions for him.

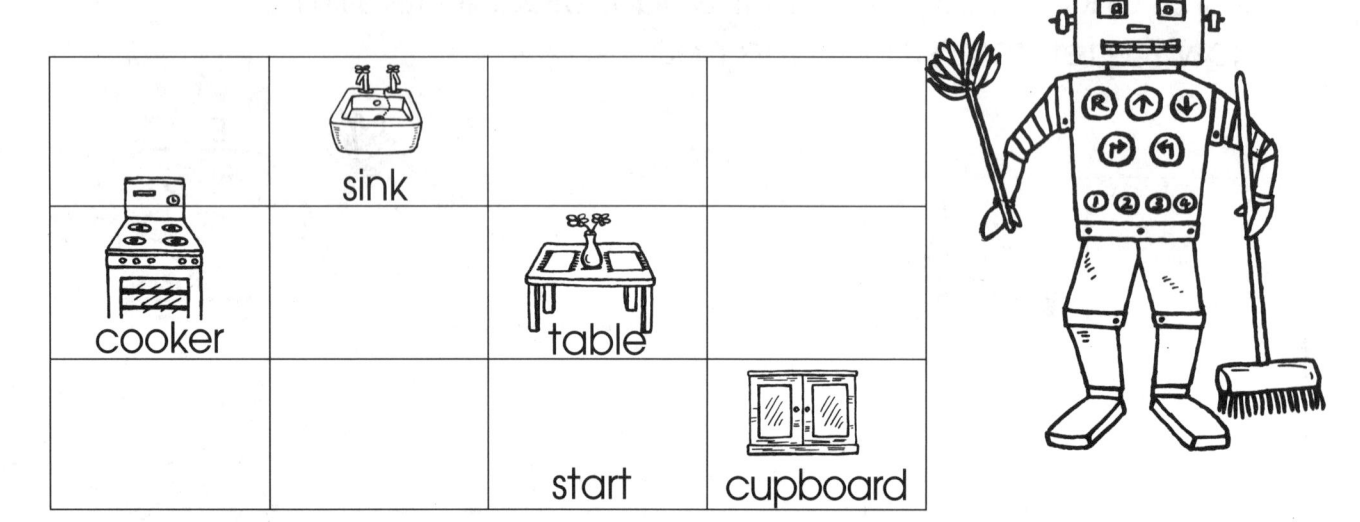

	sink		
cooker		table	
		start	cupboard

✦ Use these symbols to write your instructions.

R = repeat   ↑ = forward   ↓ = backward

↰ = left   ↱ = right

The first one has been done for you.

1. From start to cooker = ↰ 2 ↑ 1

2. From cooker to sink =

3. From start to sink =

4. From cooker to cupboard =

Name _____ Activity 3 Date _____

✦ Robby Robot ✦

✦ Help Robby Robot to clean the living room by writing the instructions for him.

bookcase				chair	lamp
		table			
television					sofa
		start			

✦ Use these symbols to write your instructions:

R = repeat   ↑ = forward   ↓ = backward

↰ = left   ↱ = right

1. From start to sofa =

2. From sofa to chair =

3. From chair to television =

4. From television to table =

5. From table to book case =

6. From lamp to start =

ICT Skills
Reception/Year 1

Photocopiable
©Hopscotch Educational Publishing
57

Lesson 14
Predicting instructions

◆ Learning objectives

+ To know that the results of instructions can be predicted.
+ To predict and test the results of instructions.

◆ Resources

+ Large open space with a grid marked as in Lesson 12.
+ Picture or word labels for pond, tree and shed.
+ Aircom CD-Rom Activity 11 (a–c).

◆ Whole class activities

+ Remind the children about the previous lesson where they wrote instructions for Robby Robot. Tell them that they are going to carry out some more activities today using instructions. Explain that today the grid is a garden. Ask three children to stand in three different squares, holding a word/picture of a tree, pond or shed. Tell the other children that some treasure has been hidden in the garden and they have to work out where it is!

+ Have a written sequence of instructions prepared (or use symbol cards) and place it where everyone can see it. Read it out to remind the children what the symbols mean. Tell them where the starting point is and the direction to face and then ask them to work out, by reading the instructions and following them in their heads, where the treasure is hidden. Is it near the tree, in the pond or under the shed? Ask them to record their prediction by writing or drawing their answers on a piece of paper.

+ Ask someone to come out and step out the instructions on the grid. Where do they end up? Ask the children to look at their piece of paper to see if their prediction was correct. The activity could be repeated several times using different instructions.
+ The children could then work in pairs or small groups with someone writing the instructions for the others to predict and test out.
+ The activity on the Aircom CD-Rom can be used as an independent task. It invites children to read some instructions and predict where a puppy is hiding. There are three different ability levels.

◆ Group activities

Activity sheets

+ The activity sheets should be used after the whole class activities. You will need to explain the activity sheets very carefully before the children commence. An adult could sit with the group to read the instructions.

◆ Plenary session

Ask someone from each group to explain what they had to do on their activity sheet. Share the responses. Did the children predict correctly? What problems did they have in testing out their predictions?

Name _____ Activity 1   Date _____

✦ Buried treasure ✦

✦ Some treasure has been buried near the tree in this garden. Put a ✔ next to the instructions you think are correct to get from the start to the tree.

Put a ✔ if you think this will lead you to the

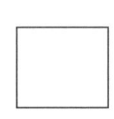

1. ↑ 2 ↱ 1 ☐

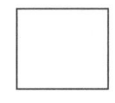

2. ↰ 1 ↑ 1 ☐

3. ↱ 1 ↑ 2 ↰ 1 ☐

↑	= forward
↰	= left
↱	= right

The garden

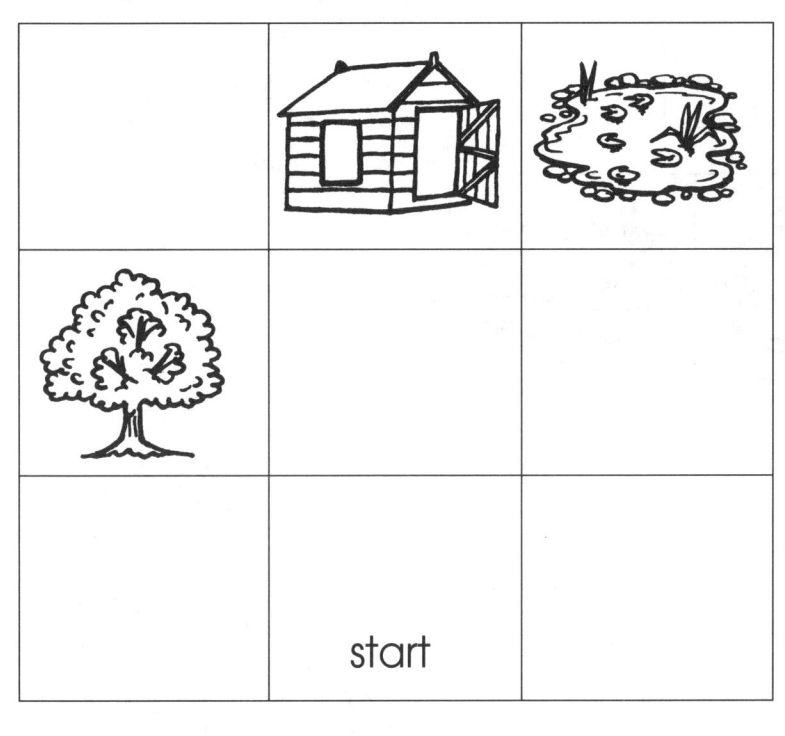

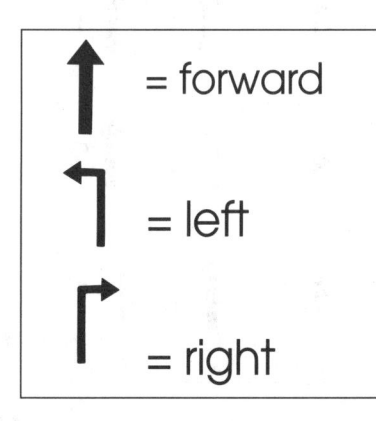

	🏠	🪴
🌳		
	start	

✦ Now draw a line on the garden to see if you are right.

ICT Skills
Reception/Year 1

59
©Hopscotch Educational Publishing

Name _____ Activity 2 Date _____

✦ Buried treasure ✦

✦ Some treasure has been buried near the tree in this garden. Put a ✔ next to the instructions you think are correct to get from start to the tree.

Put a ✔ if you think this will lead you to the

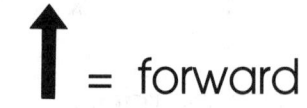

1. R2 ↑1 ☐

2. ↰1 ↑2 ↱1 ☐

3. ↰1 ↑1 ☐

4. ↱1 ↑2 ☐

5. ↑2 ↱1 ☐

R = repeat
↑ = forward
↰ = left
↱ = right

start

✦ Now draw a line on the garden to see if you are right.

Name _____   Activity 3   Date _____

✦ Buried treasure ✦

✦ Some treasure has been buried near the tree in this garden. Put a ✔ next to the instructions you think are correct to get from start to the tree.

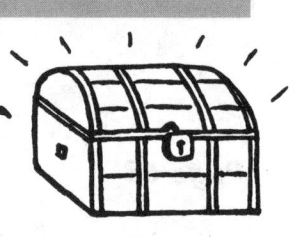

Put a ✔ if you think this will lead you to the

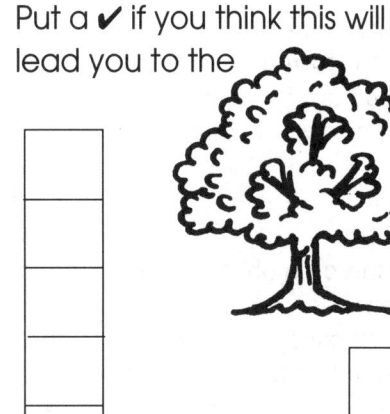

1.   ↑2   ⌐2   ↑2
2.   R2   2↑
3.   ⌐2   ↑4
4.   ↑4   ⌐1   ↓1
5.   ⌐3   ↑4
6.   ⌐1   ↑2
7.   R3   1⌐
8.   ↑4   ⌐1   ↓2

R = repeat

↑ = forward

↓ = backward

⌐ = left

⌐ = right

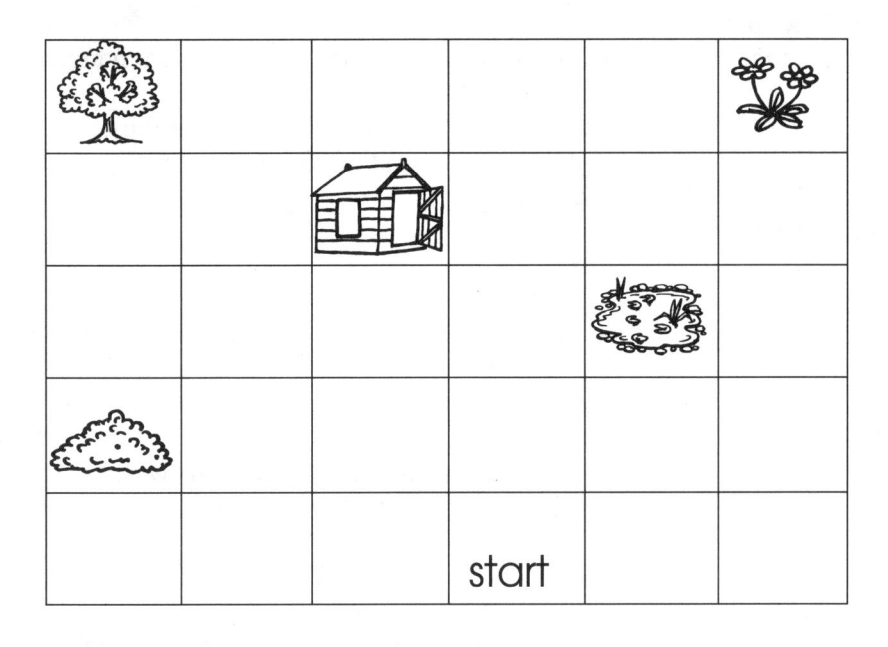

✦ Now draw a line on the garden to see if you are right.

Appendix

◆ **Suggestions for using these pages...**

Page 63

- ✦ Use these to label the computer equipment in Lesson 1.
- ✦ Photocopy several copies onto card. The children could play snap to help them learn the words.
- ✦ Mount the words on card and display as a mobile near the computer. Use this as a word bank.

Page 64

- ✦ Copy or enlarge these pictures on a photocopier to make the big book in Lesson 2.
- ✦ Photocopy, cut and mount on card. The children could use the word cards from Lesson 2 and match the pictures to the words.
- ✦ Use the pictures for story writing. Stories could be word processed and made into a book.

Page 65

- ✦ This page can be used to support and extend the activities in Lesson 4.
- ✦ Mount a copy onto card and cover with plastic. The children can use it to model how to find particular keys.
- ✦ Photocopy enough copies for a small group. Have races to see who can find particular keys the quickest (to aid key recognition).

Page 66

- ✦ This page can be used to support the activities in Lesson 4.
- ✦ Make several copies, mount on card and cut out. The children could play snap by matching upper to lower case letters.
- ✦ Use the cards to have races – how fast can the children sort them into alphabetical order or make the qwerty keyboard?

Page 67

- ✦ This page can be used to support and extend Lesson 8. The children sort the objects into as many different categories as possible.
- ✦ The children could use the pictures to make a book about household things. The text could be word processed and printed out.

Page 68

- ✦ This page is used with Lesson 9. Photocopy and cut up the foods to make cards. Put the cards into separate containers and hand them out when the children choose their favourite meal.
- ✦ They could also work in small groups and use the pictures to make their own group pictogram.

Page 69

- ✦ This page is used with the focus group in Lesson 10.
- ✦ The page could be photocopied and cut up so the children can match the words to the symbols to reinforce their knowledge.
- ✦ The children could take the page home to find machines and devices in their homes that use the same symbols. They could draw the devices and bring them to school to make a display.

Page 70

- ✦ This page is used in the whole class introduction in Lesson 11.
- ✦ It would also be a useful support for those children who need further practice in sequencing activities.

Page 71

- ✦ This page can be enlarged to use with Lesson 13.
- ✦ You could make word cards to go with these. The children could then match the symbols to the words.
- ✦ The children could use the cards to 'write' sequences for each other.

Page 72

- ✦ This is an individual record sheet for recording the skills and knowledge achieved in ICT.

computer

keyboard

mouse

monitor

disc　key

CD-ROM

drive

mat

ICT Skills
Reception/Year 1

ICT Skills
Reception/Year 1

Photocopiable
©Hopscotch Educational Publishing

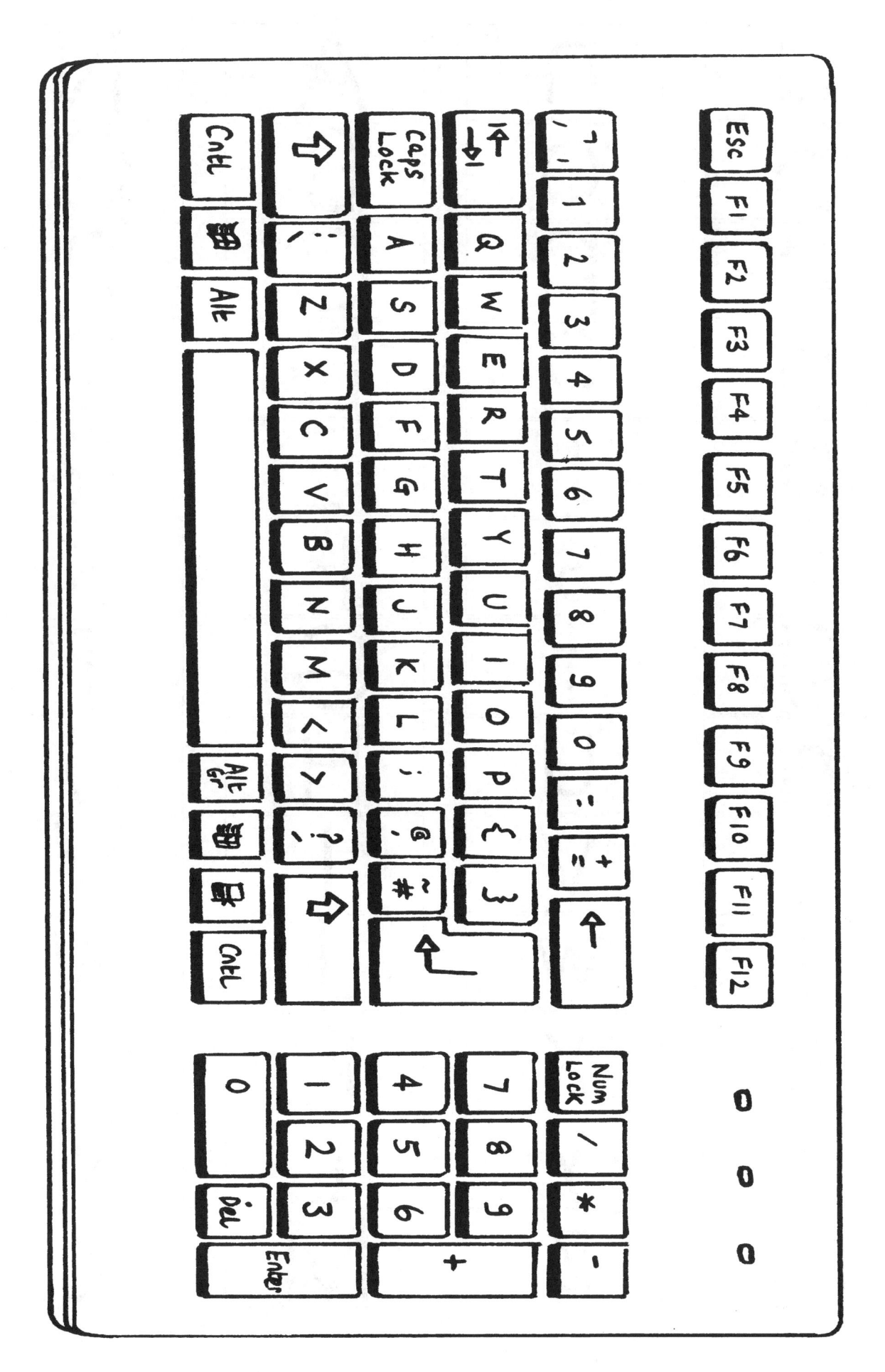

ICT Skills
Reception/Year 1

Photocopiable
©Hopscotch Educational Publishing
65

a	n	A	N
b	o	B	O
c	p	C	P
d	q	D	Q
e	r	E	R
f	s	F	S
g	t	G	T
h	u	H	U
i	v	I	V
j	w	J	W
k	x	K	X
l	y	L	Y
m	z	M	Z

ICT Skills
Reception/Year 1

Photocopiable
©Hopscotch Educational Publishing

67

ICT Skills
Reception/Year 1

Photocopiable
©Hopscotch Educational Publishing

Rec ●

Pause ‖

▶/■

▼

▼▼

▲▲

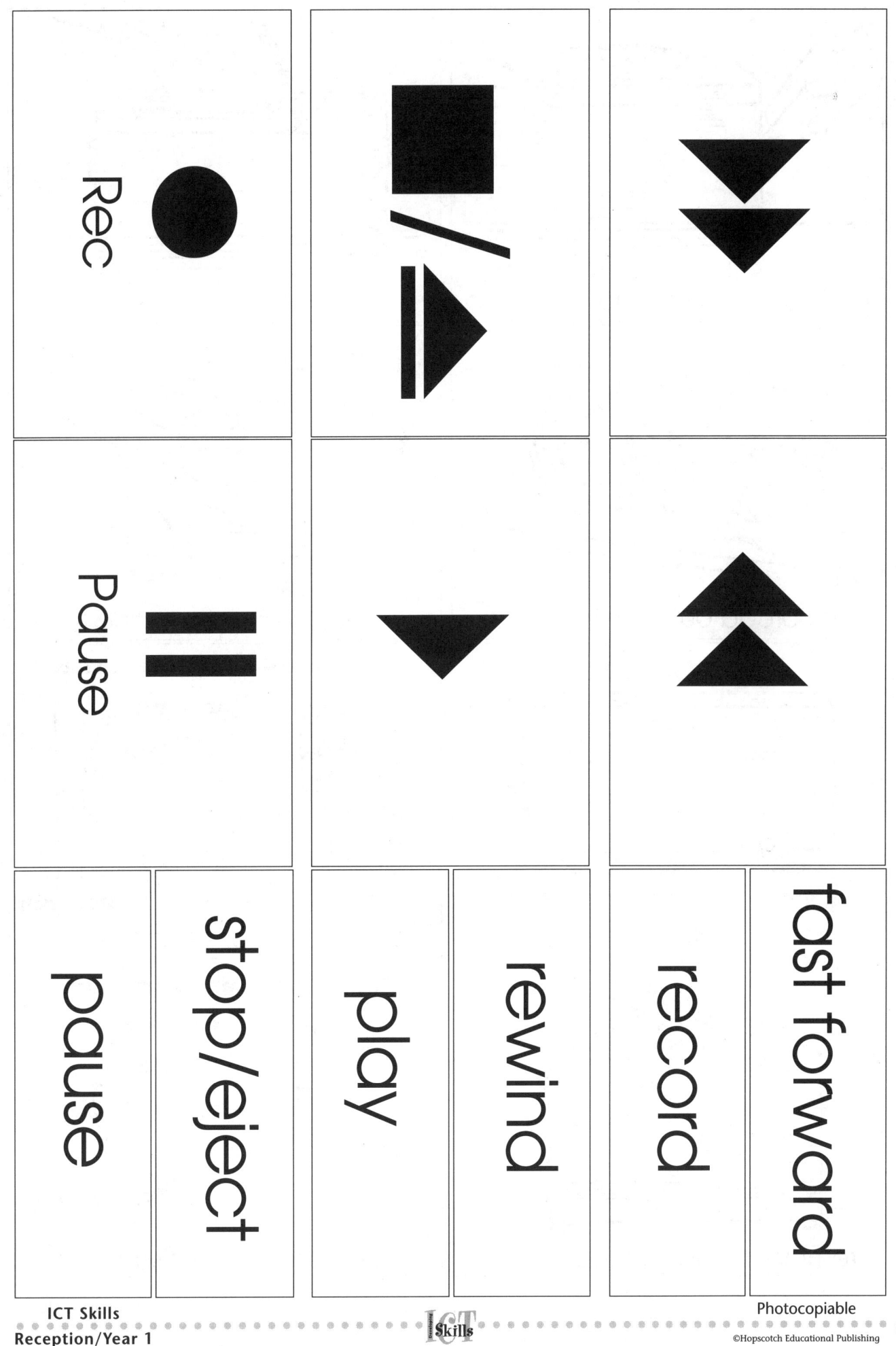

pause | **stop/eject** | **play** | **rewind** | **record** | **fast forward**

ICT Skills
Reception/Year 1

Photocopiable
©Hopscotch Educational Publishing

push lever down to lower bread	put bread into toaster
take bread out from wrapper	turn dial to select toasting level
wait for toast to pop up	turn toaster on at socket
remove toast from toaster	turn toaster off at socket

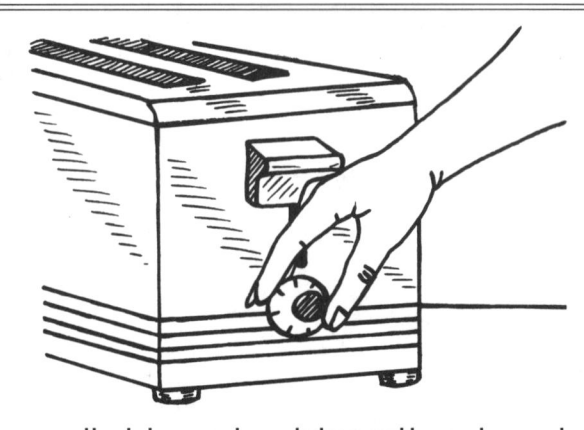

ICT Skills
Reception/Year 1

Photocopiable
©Hopscotch Educational Publishing

ICT Assessment

Name_____ Year_____ Date_____ Level_____

Tick the boxes and look for best fit when assessing level.

QCA Expectations		QCA SoW Unit		NC level
some children will not have made so much progress and will:	use software, including a simple adventure game, that represents a real or fantasy situation; create a simple representation of a real or fantasy situation with help	1A	☐	W
	enter single words from a keyboard; use a word bank to combine words, with help	1B	☐	
	have had opportunities to collect information in various forms and from various sources	1C	☐	
	use personal descriptions to describe objects	1D	☐	
	enter information into a graphing package	1E	☐	
	read a set of instructions and sometimes predict the correct outcome; produce instructions but sequence them incorrectly or make assumptions	1F	☐	
most children will:	understand that a computer can represent real or fantasy situations and that these do not replicate the original exactly; know that simple adventure games also represent real or fantasy situations; create a simple representation of a real or fantasy situation using either an objects-based graphics program or a painting program	1A	☐	1
	enter single words from a keyboard; use a word bank to assemble sentences that communicate meaning	1B	☐	
	know that information exists in a variety of forms and be able to gather it from a variety of sources	1C	☐	
	use key words to label and classify objects	1D	☐	
	use a graphing package to select appropriate icons, recognise quantities and create a pictogram	1E	☐	
	read a set of instructions and usually predict the correct outcome; produce an accurate set of instructions for others to follow	1F	☐	
some children will have progressed further and will:	use a variety of software, including adventure games, to represent real or fantasy situations and identify similarities and differences; explain their decision/choices	1A	☐	1–2
	use ICT to create sentences that communicate meaning, using the keyboard for the majority of the text	1B	☐	
	recognise that computer programs use sounds, text and pictures to convey information; begin to recognise some of the conventions used in computer programs to represent information	1C	☐	
	use key words from fixed categories to label and classify objects	1D	☐	
	use a graphing package to select appropriate icons; recognise quantities and create a pictogram; make comparisons, such as 'twice as many'	1E	☐	
	read a set of instructions and predict the correct outcome; produce an accurate set of instructions using standardised measurements and agreed language	1F	☐	

ICT Skills Reception/Year 1